On the Way to Siberia

Recollections of Anti-Aircraft Assistant
Hermann Frech, 1944-1945

Mandinam Press

First printing

Translation, historical editing and annotations: Duane A. March
Supervising Editor: Abe F. March

ISBN: 978-1-4710-8163-7
Published by Mandinam Press
www.mandinampress.co.uk

Contents

"Ohne Gefühl, keine Erinnerung."
"There is no memory without emotion."

— Hans Joachim Markowitsch , physiological psychologist and memory researcher, *Chrismon* (April 2008)

Prologue
Germany December 1943

The year 1943 marked the beginning of the end for Nazi Germany. It began with the catastrophic defeat and the surrender of approximately 107,800 soldiers of the Sixth Army in Stalingrad and continued through the surrender of all Axis forces in North Africa and the exit of Italy as a German ally after the Allied invasion of that country. Yet German forces still stood deep within the territory of the Soviet Union to the East. The western frontier – the Atlantic Ocean – still stood inviolate. The fighting in Italy was slow and brutal going for the Allies there, and the Alps threatened to block their way should they succeed in capturing the whole country.

In one sense, the war seemed far away to most Germans living at home within their borders. In another sense, the war was a daily presence in their lives, brought to them by Allied bombers that ranged the skies over Germany in increasing numbers. Their targets were for the most part larger cities and manufacturing facilities. Rural dwellers could see them overhead on their way to some near or distant population center, shake their heads in concern and pity, then return to their own worries. Many of them had fathers, brothers or sons who were fighting on some distant front. Occasionally some would visit on leave. Just as often, a family would be informed that their loved one had fallen: *Für Führer, Volk und Vaterland**. The family mourned their loss, comforted by friends, many of whom wondering when they might be visited by the same grim news. Yet they still had their children. Hopefully, the war would be over before the *Wehrmacht*** demanded their service.

Such was the situation in Göcklingen and of the Frech family. Hermann Frech, son of Friedrich (Fritz), a wine press and barrel cooper, and Emma, was born May 9th, 1928. In December 1943 he was only fifteen and a half years old, and the prospect of war service must

* "For Fuehrer, People and Fatherland"

**The *Wehrmacht* was the collective term for all armed forces in Germany. Each service had its own designation: *Heer* (army), Luftwaffe (air force), *Kriegsmarine* (navy).

have seemed still distant. Yet already in January 1943 his family would have cause to fear for him. A decree was issued on January 22nd, 1943 concerning *Kriegshilfseinsatz der Jugend bei der Luftwaffe* ("War Auxiliary Deployment of Youth into the Luftwaffe"). The order called for drafting whole school classes with male students born in 1926 and 1927 into a military corps, supervised by Hitler Youth and Luftwaffe personnel. This led to the *Luftwaffenhelfer* ("Luftwaffe assistant") program that addressed the increasing threat posed by Allied bombing raids and Germany's need for soldiers, especially on the Eastern Front.

Deployment included ideological indoctrination by the Hitler Youth, military duties and limited continuation of the normal school curriculum, often by the original teachers. Thus, adolescents would replace adult anti-aircraft personnel, freeing them for frontline combat service. Approximately sixty-eight thousand pupils were thus made eligible for this auxiliary military service*.

In addition to the age-groups affected, there were two other stipulations of the War Auxiliary Deployment decree: the boys were to serve near their hometowns, and girls were not required to serve (although they could volunteer once they were sixteen years old).

All three stipulations would be amended later. Girls were eventually conscripted for duty in the communications and signals service** and on air searchlights. Later, female members of the *Reichsarbeitsdient* (Reich Labor Service) were deployed to anti-aircraft batteries. As we shall see, boys were eventually deployed at anti-aircraft installations far from home.

The boys conscripted into this service would come to be known as the Flak Helper Generation. These "child soldiers," scarred by their experiences, yet unburdened by complicity in Nazi crimes, became pacifist and decidedly anti-fascist. Many contributed significantly to Germany's reconstruction and renewal after the war.

Perhaps the most famous among them is Pope Benedict XVI, born Joseph Alois Ratzinger in 1927. He was deployed at an installation near Munich meant to protect the BMW works (BMW also manufactured military vehicles). He was eventually conscripted into the Reich Labor Service and sent to eastern Austria until taken prisoner by US forces.

Nobel Laureate Günter Grass (Prize for Literature: *The Tin Drum*), also born in 1927, served as a Flak Helper until he was conscripted into the *Waffen SS* (10th SS-Panzer-Division "Frundsberg") in November 1944 at the age of seventeen.

---

*The source for many of these statistics is the German Wikipedia article, http://de.wikipedia.org/wiki/Flakhelfer

**They were called *Blitzmädels* ("Lightning Girls").

Hans-Dietrich Genscher, later German Foreign Minister (1974-1992), a man who would essentially steer Germany's international relations, began his military service as a Flak Helper in 1943 before being conscripted first into the Reich Labor Service (1944) and then volunteering for the army in 1945 in order to avoid conscription into the SS. As a part of "Wenck's Army" (12th Army) he took part in a vain effort to break through the Soviet encirclement of Berlin in April 1945 before his capture by US soldiers and transfer to a British POW camp.

Claus von Amsberg, German diplomat and later Prince Consort of Queen Beatrix of the Netherlands, was born in 1926 and served as a Flak Helper as a navy auxiliary from 1942 to 1944 until he was conscripted into the army (90th Panzer Grenadier Division) and sent to Italy where he was taken prisoner by US forces.

Manfred Rommel, son of the famous Field Marshal Erwin Rommel (the "Desert Fox"), and later Mayor of Stuttgart (1974-1996) was born in 1928. When his father was forced to commit suicide in the aftermath of the July 20th 1944 plot to kill Adolf Hitler, Manfred had to appear at his father's very public funeral in October 1944 clad in his Flak Helper uniform, knowing full well how his father had died. He later said in an interview with the newspaper *Die Zeit* in 2002, "To this day I still have a nightmare from my time as a Luftwaffe Auxiliary." He eventually deserted and surrendered himself to the French First Army.

As the year 1943 drew to a close, eleven months since the decree was issued, a whole new age-group was nearly a year older.

North Sea
DENMARK
Baltic Sea
Königsberg (Kaliningrad)
Danzig (Gdansk)
East Prussia
Hamburg
Elbe R.
Bremen
Weser R.
Oder R.
Soviet Forces ca. 1 January 1945
Küstrin (Kostrzyn nad Odra)
Landsberg an der Warthe (Gorzow Wielkopolski)
Prison Camp
Berlin
Seelow Heights
Frankfurt / Oder
Warsaw
Weichsel R.
Posen (Poznań)
Warthe R.
POLAND
NETHERLANDS
Hanover
Elbe R.
Oder R.
Breslau (Wrocław)
Silesia
Cologne
Aachen
BELGIUM
GERMANY
End of December 1944
Saxony
Dresden
Radebeul
Most (Brüx)
Rhine R.
Frankfurt
Hanau
Mainz
Main R.
Darmstadt
LUXEMBURG
Ludwigshafen
Mannheim
Palatinate
Landau
Bohemia
Prague
CZECHOSLOVAKIA
Soviet Forces ca. 1 January 1945
Bavaria
Allied Forces ca. 1 January 1945
Karlsruhe
ALSACE
Strasbourg
Danube
Danube
Bavaria
Isar R.
Lech R.
Munich
Linz
Vienna
Danube
FRANCE
Rhine R.
Menzenschwand
Schongau
Zürich
SWITZERLAND
OSTMARK (Austria)
Outward Trek
Homeward
Germany's Eastern Borders
internationally recognized 1938, including
Sudetenland
Austria (renamed Ostmark)

Chapter 1

Flak Helper – Early 1944

It is December, 1943, and the last day of school before Christmas vacation. Dr. Petri, the head schoolmaster, enters the classroom of grade 8b. There is total silence. There has to be a reason when the "King" comes by personally.

"I have to tell you," he begins with a slight nasal voice, "that after your Christmas vacation, you will not be returning to school since you are going to be called up to serve at the homeland anti-aircraft installation in Ludwigshafen. I hope that you will fulfill your duty and bring honor to the school during this difficult time."

There was no cheering, only silence and anxious anticipation. Everyone was determined to be a "man," to the extent that one can speak of fifteen to sixteen year-old boys as being men. The names of the students are read out loud. Those born in 1929 and one Swiss student are not on the list. They will remain behind. All others are to report for duty on January 10th, 1944.

However, it turns out quite differently. After we arrive at school following our Christmas vacation, we are sent home again. We are told that "something had happened" at the anti-aircraft battery where we were supposed to go, and that they would not be able to take us. We later learned that during the heavy bombing attack of December 30th, 1943, the battery's range-finding post had also been bombed. Four anti-aircraft helpers* from the "Gymnasium** at the Kaiser Dom" in Speyer had paid for their induction with their lives.

A new induction order is issued for February 10th, 1944. It stipulates that in the meantime we will spend one week at the town of Menzenschwand (in the southern Black Forest) in military training.

---

*These boys were officially named Luftwaffenhelfer (Air Force Auxiliaries), more commonly Flakhelfer (Flak or Anti-Aircraft Helpers)

**College prep secondary school (US: "high school")

Mountain infantry soldiers there try to teach us to ski. In spite of the cold, the days that we spend in this heavily snowed-in, peaceful valley are the last ones in which we would still be able to laugh and be happy.

In February, we move to the anti-aircraft battery that lies north of Oppau in the region called Petersau*. The battery consists of six 8.8 cm caliber anti-aircraft guns, and one range-finding post with a radar and range-finding unit that calculates the necessary data to be passed on to the artillery. There is an additional 8.8 cm anti-aircraft position to the north of us and a heavier 10.5 cm battery to the southwest. All together they provide protection for BASF (the German chemical company**) from attacks coming from the northwest.

At the 8.8 cm anti-aircraft post

*A flood plain located between Ludwigshafen and Frankenthal near the west bank of the Rhine.

**Still to this day a globally recognized pharmaceutical company.

We are ordered to fall in and line up according to height. First Lieutenant Lentz, who heads the battery, greets us. We are then divided into two groups. The taller ones will go to the artillery squadron, and the shorter ones, about the last third, to the range-finding squadron. Walls of earth that serve as shrapnel protection surround the artillery posts and our living quarters. The kitchen, medical area, locker room and the canteen, which also serves as an instruction room, are located between the artillery posts and the range-finding squadron.

We are given uniforms. They are similar to the usual air force uniforms: blue-gray in color and very much like the cut of the Hitler Youth ski uniforms. We are still wearing their swastika armbands. We line up in front of the barracks to have our pictures taken for our military IDs.

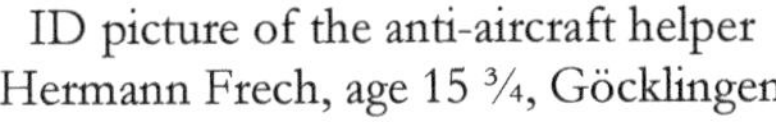

ID picture of the anti-aircraft helper Hermann Frech, age 15 ¾, Göcklingen

… and after 1 year

By today's standards, we were without a doubt, "child-soldiers." The vintner Karl Silbernagel from Göcklingen, whose son was killed in Russia, gave his opinion: "Hitler is now enlisting children for the war. Someone should put a stop to this criminal!" If his comment had become public, he would have paid for it with his life.

We are told that instruction will take place every morning. Instructor Janzer comes to the battery for this purpose. In addition, there is also an older man from Ludwigshafen who teaches biology and chemistry. However, in reality, it is often different. Postponement of our instruction becomes the norm as evidenced by the following bombing attacks (1944):

July 31st	day time air raids	500	American bombers
August 15th	" "	400	" "
August 17th	night time air raids	25	Mosquitoes, light British bombers
August 26th	" "	50	" "
September 3rd	day time air raids	500	American bombers
September 5th	" "	400	" "
September 9th	" "	400	" "

This last bombing attack consisted of 1,600 high-explosive bombs, 800 phosphorous bombs, and 25,000 incendiary bombs. There were a total of 639 air raid alerts in the area of Ludwigshafen.

A particularly heavy attack took place on Whitsunday 1944. During the night, thirty Mosquitoes (light British bombers) attacked and dropped thirty-one high-explosive bombs. The next day, the main attack followed: 400 heavy American bombers, the so-called "Flying Fortresses."

It is a sunny, spring day, with a clear blue sky. Formation upon formation appears over the forested Haardt hills to the West and flies toward us. The stream of planes never seems to end. The air vibrates, shaking from 1,600 airplane motors. We are shaking too. Finally the anti-aircraft batteries begin to shoot. The first plane is hit, and releases its bombs right in front of our position. The plane's crew follows, floating down under white parachutes.

Our classmate and medic Gustav Kuntz has a rifle pressed into his hands and is sent to the fields near Eppstein with a senior medic ("Sani"*) in order to gather up the American troops. After the attack, when we see the prisoners at the medical field station, we are amazed how tall they are and how beautiful their uniforms are. A dud bomb from one of the planes that was hit fell on the Plexiglas of our range-finding post right in front of me.

*"Sani" is short for *Sanitäter* (German for medic).

Command or range-finding post: a type of mechanical computer

Oh, if only they had merely dropped duds instead of live bombs. During 124 bombing attacks on Ludwigshafen, there were 461 aerial mine bombs, 39,688 high-explosive bombs, 46,688 phosphorous bombs and 757,696 incendiary bombs. This resulted in 1,778 deaths and 2,962 injuries. Approximately 1,000 forced laborers were not counted*.

We are not allowed into the bunkers or air-raid shelters, and simply have to endure the attacks in simple trenches.

H. Frech, Oppau/Petersau 1944

*Source: City archives Ludwigshafen.

At the radar post in front of Oggersheim:
It does not function when metal radar deflection strips (chaff) are dropped.
Hermann Frech – far left in both photos (above and below)

Chapter 2

Flak Helper – Late 1944

In the summer of 1944, the battery is moved from Oppau in the north to Oggersheim in the West, the direction from which most of the bombing formations originate. At this time, we are experiencing the heaviest attacks on BASF and Ludwigshafen.

When we arrive, the battery position is still under construction, which leaves us feeling somewhat uneasy. In spite of all difficulties, instruction in German, Latin, history, geography, mathematics, physics, chemistry and biology continue. On July 13th, 1944, we receive our yearly school reports. Our instructor, Mr. Janzer, the head of the school, Dr. Petri, and head of the battery, First Lieutenant Lenz, sign them. This ANTI-AIRCRAFT HELPER SCHOOL REPORT states that we "have been promoted to the 6th (sic) grade of the secondary school in Landau on the basis of our conduct and educational achievements." It is the last school report issued to us in the Third Reich.

The battery is losing its personnel. The anti-aircraft soldiers who are still present are ordered to the front. The soldiers (K3) that load the artillery cannons are the most indispensable; they are specially selected, strong men.

A shell weighing about 40 kg* has to be loaded by the K3 and fired within 2.5 to 3 seconds, at a rather steep trajectory. During heavy attacks, 200 firings per cannon are not unusual. Only men suitable for the job can carry out this enormous physical exertion. Supplying the cannons with ammunition is done by Russian prisoners of war belonging to the battery: men who probably volunteered for this task out of hunger or necessity.

---

*About 88 lbs. The main anti-aircraft artillery piece employed was the famous 88 mm.

Our move from Oppau to Oggersheim

Our battery assembles at the canteen. We are told that under the present situation, we have to count on forced worker uprisings in the area of Ludwigshafen, whose numbers are in the thousands. We receive machine guns for our and the battery's protection. Some of us also receive instruction in their use.

At the machine gun

We are told that the battalion commander, a major, will be conducting an inspection. He finally appears – a respectable, elderly gentleman. The inspection of the post is brief, followed by assembly of the troops at the canteen. The major begins: "You are here to defend western culture. What is culture...?"

Yes, what is culture? It is certainly not what we have been experiencing here every day. A type of instruction begins, and in between there is advice and some short discourses, (the major was probably a teacher at a secondary school with emphasis in the classics). Then, an air-raid alert: everyone runs to the anti-aircraft emplacements and to the various location and range-finding posts. We quietly name the "un-culture" barbarism as it continues its progression.

Hermann Frech, Karl Henrich, Bruno Klein

October 1944 – At the command post
Far left Brüno Klein and Hermann Frech

The fighting to the west draws closer and closer. All those involved with the battery have to commit themselves in writing to defend it to the last man. In anticipation of the expected land battle, the battery is additionally outfitted with anti-tank ammunition. For those of us who are anti-aircraft helpers, instruction of the infantry anti-tank weapon (*Panzerfaust*)* becomes an important part of the so-called "land battle school"**. It was developed for close combat against armored vehicles.

Christmas 1944

Panzerfaust is the German version of the "bazooka"
***Erdkampfschul*

Christmas 1944: the Americans have already reached Hagenau and Weissenburg[*], and are targeting Landau with their artillery.

The Palatinate (*die Pfalz*) in south-western Germany

We have become more serious and fear the future and what will happen at home. The attacks of the fighter bombers ("Jabos"[**]) do not let up. Presently, there is only one "proper soldier" (E1[***]) left at the command post. He calculates the distance to the enemy planes by looking through a telescopic sight and placing a row of five diamond shaped symbols so that they cover the target, thereby gauging height and distance. The optically determined values are immediately entered into a mechanical steering unit (a simple type of computer) and then passed on to the artillery, so that the firing personnel can set the timings. His job demanded very good visual judgment (he also had to gauge how far the aircraft would fly by the time the gun crew fired and the projectile would fly before reaching target.)

---

[*] *Haguenau* and *Wissembourg* are the French spellings.

[**] "Jabo" is a short form for *Jagdbomber* (fighter bomber).

[***] Up to this point, the "E1" was always a soldier, not an auxiliary. Auxiliaries were now to be trained to take over this function.

I begin my service as an E4. It is my duty to predict the flight path of a flying target based on its current course. This, to be sure, involves some guesswork; an aircraft's path – whether straight or turning –could change at any moment. Whenever that happens, my superior screams at me, "Frech! What the hell are you doing!" or some similar expression of displeasure.

The E2 and E3 orient the range-finding unit vertically and horizontally. Now the E1 is also to be replaced by an anti-aircraft helper. To that effect, two of us, Paul Ullemeyer from Queichheim and Hermann Frech from Göcklingenare ordered to go to the anti-aircraft artillery school in Schongau in the middle of January 1945.

We have all changed during the last year; have become more serious and more mature. Boys, one could almost say "brats," have become serious young men. However, some of us will not survive the beginning of 1945.

Werner Deck (Dammheim) and Erhart Hatzenbühler (Offenbach) at the radar post. Hatzenbühler, on the right, was killed in 1945*.

*I thank Bruno Klein, Carl Heupel and Dr. Mörz from the State Archives of Ludwigshafen for their support in the form of notes, explanations and photographs. (Hermann Frech)

Chapter 3

Leaving Home – Winter/Spring 1945

In January, 1945, the war entered its last phase. The last great German offensive, the Ardennes Offensive (or "Battle of the Bulge") had been defeated, and the Western Allies resumed their inexorable advance on Germany's western frontier. In the East, German forces had somehow been able to slow down the Soviet advance. On January 17th, however, the Soviets finally took Warsaw and then promptly launched a broad offensive along the entire Eastern Front. The dam broke. Within a week, Soviet troops had crossed into Germany proper in East Prussia and in Silesia*. By April, they would be knocking on the gates of Berlin.

While people like Hermann Frech were away from home, their families and friends increasingly had to deal with deaths, bombing raids and shortages of all kinds. The Frech family was, however, comparatively fortunate to live in a rural area of small military importance and gifted with fertile soil. The residents of Göcklingen and neighboring towns were able grow and raise their own food, and the nearby Palatinate Forest supplied wood fuel for the winter.

In school, but a different kind of school

An anti-aircraft position located near Oggersheim. What is the purpose of constant calculations by a command post or an optical range-calculating post attached to a mechanical-type computer? It instantly conveys the derived values to the artillery units, so that the anti-aircraft helpers in that location can set the necessary advance timing on the shell fuses. Again and again we have to adjust our benchmark settings to the church tower of Eppstein. To our good fortune, it is not cold for January. The temperatures are more those in March.

*An excellent source for this situation and events of the year 1945 is Richard Bessel's *Germany 1945: From War to Peace*. Simon and Schuster: London, 2009.

We are told to go into a totally darkened room. After a few minutes we come out into the brightness of a sunny day. How long does it take one to recognize letters and read numbers? That is the question. This procedure determines your degree of night vision. Finally the battery commander, First Lieutenant Lenz, announces that the anti-aircraft helpers Paul Ullemer and Hermann Frech have received the best results and will be dispatched the next day to the anti-aircraft artillery school at Schongau in order to be instructed as range finding personnel. Up to this time, this function had been performed by anti-aircraft soldiers.

Paul and I receive our marching orders. We also receive a half loaf of commissary bread and half a salami sausage. We set out toward the train station in Frankenthal on foot. We would never see our battery or our classmates again.

Traveling mostly at night, we begin our adventure on a train ride to the wintry Allgäu*. The journey takes us through heavily damaged train stations and past destroyed cities. After two days and numerous stops due to fighter-bomber attacks, we reach the little city of Schongau, which has an elevation of over 2,000 feet. It lies peacefully on the left bank of the Lech River and has never been bombed. From the train station, we head to the anti-aircraft artillery school located on a slope above the town.

The anti-aircraft school is beautifully situated. It consists of a collection of several buildings constructed of light sandstone, in the "Adolf Hitler School" style, similar to a mediaeval castle fort. The domed slope is covered with snow, just like the rest of the Allgäu Mountain range; add to this, blue sky and the snow-covered peaks of the Alps. The warm sunrays feel good and give the illusion of a peaceful, idyllic place, except for all those artillery and calculating stands around the site.

After the normal signing-in in the orderly room, Paul and I are directed to a detail of anti-aircraft helpers for instruction in range-calculation. A detail consists of about thirty persons, which roughly corresponds to a schoolroom class. A sergeant heads our detail. He is from Austria, and he has us march and sing whenever possible, but he has his troubles with us. One time, when we were not singing loudly or beautifully enough for him, he shouted, "All of you, to the left in quick-time." We ran from the street over a snow-covered meadow and did not heed his command. "About face!" he commanded as loudly as

---

*A region in southern Bavaria at the foot of the Alps.

he could, but we intentionally ran on and into a wide brook, which was, however, only knee-deep. "Back, back!" he shouted. So we slowly walked back to the street in our soaking-wet shoes. He pleaded with us to sneak back to our quarters and not let officers catch us, and to make sure that we dry our feet well so that none of us would get sick. And then we were told to stay quietly in our rooms until supper. We had achieved what we had wanted. By the way, the food was not bad at all during that time period.

We are told that calculating practice will take place tomorrow morning, since no fighter-bombers and no bomber squadrons are to be seen. They usually come over the Alps from Italy in order to attack Munich or Augsburg. A German Arado plane flies in above us; sometimes higher, sometimes lower. Occasionally a Messerschmitt 262 thunders above us from the nearby airport at Fürstenfeldbruck. It is the first production jet plane in the world, very fast and impressive. One of us has to calculate the distance, convey the distance value to a second person via a pipe-whistle, while a third person immediately enters the data into a special notebook. Simultaneously, the distance to the plane is determined by radar. In the afternoon, we all sit in a makeshift lecture room. The values determined by radar are read to us: 4550…4560…4580… That's what we hear from the podium, while we concentrate on writing these numbers next to those determined by us.

Then the evaluation begins. Sometimes we are off by 30 feet, then by 180 feet, 600 feet or even more. That happened to my neighbor. He was from Thorn in West Prussia and I can still hear him whining. "No matter what I do, I can't improve!" But I am very good, so in the beginning of March 1945, I am ordered to an anti-aircraft position near Hanover, together with another anti-aircraft helper, a corporal and a non-commissioned officer. The battery to be constructed there will use rockets to fight off the bombing formations intended for Berlin.

To the North, to the South and again to the North

After many delays, we arrive at the main train station in Hanover. The night is pitch-black. Because of the many fighter-bombers, the trains only run at night. The sirens sound. It's an air raid alert. Get out of the train station quickly! We run, seek, ask and get safely into an air raid shelter, just in the nick of time. "Oh my God, are you tanned!" comments one woman.

Another one asks, “Are you from Africa or Italy?”

“No, from the sunny Allgäu,” is our answer. We had not noticed how healthy we looked, thanks to the fresh air, the good milk and the fine cheese of the Allgäu.

This time the bomber formations fly over Hanover in order to release their load on the city of Wolfsburg, which lies further to the East. After two hours, we are walking through the bombed ruins of Hanover. It is almost dawn when we reach the anti-aircraft position. In the daylight we can see that it lies along the Mittellandkanal* (Midland Canal). We were expected, but they don’t know what to do with us. We are bored. We sit on the bank of the canal and look into the water. Not far away is a shot-up barge from which the inhabitants of a nearby village carry away cartons and backpacks full of cans filled with vegetables and meat. They were probably destined for Berlin. In the evening, three girls arrive from the village. They sit with us and we talk. The next evening, they return and bring cakes. Will they visit us again? We don’t know; there aren’t any rockets, but the Americans are coming closer and closer. Therefore we leave. We are transferred to a unit in Brüx**, Czechoslovakia.

What happens now is an adventure. Travel to Dresden is in small stages, mostly at night, progressing very slowly. Then, the totally over-filled train stops. A smell of something burning fills the air. Dresden has just been heavily bombed. We hear that it has been totally reduced to rubble, and that passing through it is impossible and prohibited. Unbelievably, we are able to travel a short distance by streetcar. What I have always wondered about, even to this day, and later also in Berlin, is that there is still electric power. The streetcar stops. It is noon. I cut a large slice from my commissary bread loaf and take a little of the summer sausage. The rest I pack up, put in my knapsack and go outside like the others. Where are we? I read: Radebeul. I’ve heard that name before. This is where Karl May*** lived. Since our stay was longer than expected, I walk to the next house, but it is closed. Through the window I see various Indian tools. I go back and am missing the bread and sausage, our rations for the next four days. Stolen! In my naïve belief in the decency of the German “national common interest,” I had thought that this would be an impossibility!

We start walking. Our group still consists of a corporal, our non-commissioned officer, who has our marching orders, and us two anti-

---

*This canal is Germany’s longest, running from the Rhine River valley (via the Dortmund-Ems Canal) to the Weser River and then past Hanover before connecting to the Elbe River near Magdeburg.

**English: Most, a town about 77 km northwest of Prague.

***Karl May was a 19th century German author, most famous for his tales of the American West.

aircraft helpers. And so we walk, walk and walk, always in the direction of the *Erzgebirge*[*]. On the way, we are shot at by fighter-bombers. We jump from the right-hand street ditch to the left one and back again, until it stops. We are increasingly tormented by thirst. We are happy for every village well, where we drink until we are full and can wash our faces. But after the thirst is gone, we get even hungrier. We have not eaten in days and now we are starving. I stop at a house with low windows, knock on the window and wait. An old, wretched woman answers. I ask for a slice of bread and offer her my overalls. She shakes her head and closes the window. Still hungry, I continue on, leaving my overalls by the window.

Since I haven't been able to change my underwear for weeks now, I begin to get sores between my legs. We stop at a pharmacy in a small town. I count my money and am able to scrape together ten Reichsmarks. The friendly old pharmacist makes me a present of some cream, which does give me a little relief. We move on. After a while we hear the sound of a truck behind us. The non-commissioned officer waves and the military vehicle stops. What luck! The driver says that he is on the way to Brüx! Unfortunately, he only has room for two of us, but says that another car would be coming along soon. They always stay a certain distance apart for fear of the fighter-bombers. And indeed, a second car does arrive. Since the non-commissioned officer and an anti-aircraft helper got into the first car, the corporal and I get into the second one, and in order to keep a certain distance, continue on after waiting five minutes.

It is night time when we arrive in Brüx, called "Most" in Czech. Brüx is situated in the brown coal region, on the south side of the Erzgebirge, an industrial city the size of Landau. At that time, of the 36,000 inhabitants, 16,000 were Germans from the Sudetenland[**].

We get out at an intersection and wait. It is cold and damp and the air smells of burned briquettes from the many stoves burning brown coal. A military vehicle approaches and stops. I wonder if they know how to get to the anti-aircraft barracks. Two men get out. Military Police! You can recognize them by the silver disk, hanging on a chain. It is half as large as a flat plate.

"Your marching orders!" he demands.

"Our section leader has them," we reply.

"Everyone we catch says that. You're under arrest. Get in!"

---

[*]The Ore Mountains, which form the boundary between German Saxony and Czech Bohemia

[**]The Sudetenland was a region in Czechoslovakia bordering Germany and Austria. Dominated by ethnic Germans, Hitler succeeded in having it incorporated into Germany in 1938. After 1945 it was restored to Czechoslovakia, and its German inhabitants were forcibly expelled.

We are driven through the dark night in Brüx and end up at the inner courtyard of a prison. There are already a number of others belonging to the military there, as well as Czech resistance fighters in brown uniforms. We are separated and put into a cell with bunk beds. Lights out. There is no thought of sleep. I wonder what will happen to us. "Tomorrow morning we will be court-martialed for desertion," someone says in the darkness.

"And then?"

"Then we will be shot. General Schörner is in charge in Czechoslovakia. He has issued the order of the day that all deserters are to be shot immediately. Never hear of it?"

There is silence. Sleep is out of the question. I am lying down and have pretty much come to terms with my life. I think about my parents, my grandma, about Göcklingen, my childhood girlfriend Liesel, pray and think of hymns that I know. It is after midnight and suddenly, there are steps in the hall, the sound of a cell door being opened, a light comes on, a security guard appears and our first lieutenant is standing next to him. He spent the whole night looking for us everywhere. Quickly we get off our plank-beds, grab our knapsacks and run to the anti-aircraft barracks, where he had waited for us.

Finally, finally we get some coffee and food. The next two days are spent in the barracks, where we can wash ourselves and even get clean underwear and socks. What a delight! However, our enjoyment is cut short because we receive marching orders to go to Berlin. "Transferred to an anti-aircraft battery in Berlin-Neukölln," that's what it says in black and white. Luckily, I have no idea of what's in store for me.

Chapter 4

Berlin – April 1945

While Hermann Frech made his way to Berlin his home had already fallen to US forces. During February and March, 1945, the town was subjected to frequent fighter-bomber attacks*, undoubtedly all part of the preparations for Operation Undertone**, which was launched against and across the Westwall fortifications that ran along the frontier with Alsace on 15th March, 1945. The US 7th and French 1st armies thrust northeast towards the Rhine on a front from Saarbrücken in the West to Hagenau in the Southeast. On March 20th, the US 14th Armored Division attacked through a gap at Weissenburg and drove northeast towards Bad Bergzabern. On the same day Göcklingen fell under artillery fire.

> The town's populace fled into bunkers or their own cellars. "Four nights long even the cellars of the pastor's house were filled with people from the lower town." The shell fire landed mostly in the *Hauptstrasse* (main street), where many houses lost their roofs***.

American forces fought a bitter battle with the German XC Corps for two days at Steinfeld (March 20th-22nd). Until US forces broke through on the 23rd on their way to Landau.

On the morning of March 23rd, around 11 am, retreating German soldiers blew up the bridges over the Kaiserbach stream in the Welsgasse and the Schulgasse (streets that led to each bridge), despite efforts by the townsfolk to prevent it: the streams were so insignificant as to pose no hindrance to the advancing Americans. White flags were

---

*Dr. A. Schirmer, Göcklingen bei Landau/Pfalz. Gemeindeverwaltung der Ortsgemeinde 76831 Göcklingen: 1981, pp. 151, 802-3.

**See "Operation Undertone," http://en.wikipedia.org/wiki/Operation_Undertone

****Ibid.*, p. 802.

raised that same afternoon. A squad of SS soldiers attempted to prevent Göcklingen from capitulating and made a search for German soldiers in hiding. Towards evening, the SS had withdrawn and American soldiers entered the town. They would occupy the town for about four weeks*.

By the 24th, the last German troops able to do so had withdrawn across the Rhine. The Palatinate, along with Göcklingen, was now under Allied occupation.

Meanwhile, on the Eastern Front, the Red Army had reached the Oder River and began crossing it on 16th April. The German army, in a desperate effort to hold the Soviets back from Berlin, dug in along the Seelow Heights and put up fierce resistance. Approximately one million Soviet soldiers with more than 20,000 tanks threw themselves at an estimated 110,000 Germans with 1,200 tanks. The artillery duel could be heard in Berlin sixty kilometers to the West. By the time the Germany gave way on April 19th, they left behind over 12,000 killed against approximately 33,000 Soviet dead.

On April 20th, the Soviets began an artillery bombardment of Berlin that would not stop until Berlin capitulated. On April 23rd, General Helmuth Weidling was given command of Berlin's defense. He had approximately 45,000 soldiers at his disposal, supplemented by about 40,000 *Volkssturm* as well as Hitler Youth units. The Soviets, with about 1.5 million soldiers, began their assault on the city, entering from the East as well as encircling the city to the North and South. By April 24th, the city was for all practical purposes completely surrounded.

I no longer remember how we got to Berlin. Bombed train stations and refugees from the East can be seen everywhere. Our ride on the train is mostly done at night; the carriages overflowing with people. And then we wait and wait. Unaware, we have reached the outskirts of Berlin. It is the middle of April, 1945. We wait for the express commuter, which is actually still functioning. There is heavy, muffled rumbling in the air. "That's the artillery from the front! The Russians have already reached the Oder River," someone says.

"No way," someone else answers, "they're just holding artillery exercises with anti-aircraft guns." The anti-aircraft posts are holding

---

**Ibid.*, p. 803

artillery exercises? And to think we had to save shells and weren't even allowed to shoot at returning bombers!

The first lieutenant knows his way around Berlin. He says that we are not going to the anti-aircraft battery. He has a sweetheart here, a beautiful woman. She has such a small waist that he can touch his fingers when he puts his hands around her. Perhaps we'll also get something to eat. We are told to keep our traps shut.

Finally, we find the apartment building. It has several floors and is undamaged. The young woman is obviously surprised and somewhat fearful as all four of us enter her kitchen, one at a time. The first lieutenant explains things to her. She is happy to see him and serves us some malt coffee* and bread. The lovebirds disappear into the bedroom, and we lie down to sleep on the kitchen floor. Since we have left the window open due to this extremely warm April, the night time rumbling of the artillery appears louder. Suddenly, there is loud knocking on the front door.

"Open up," someone shouts. We all wake up. The young woman comes from the bedroom into the kitchen, puts her finger on her lips, goes to the front door and opens it.

"Field Police**," we hear from behind the door, in a tone that is not pleasant.

I'm thinking: *Oh my God, Not again!* He asks if there are any anti-aircraft soldiers here and if so, if he can speak with the troop leader. The troop leader appears, shows him our marching orders and explains that we were not able to find the battery at night, but that we would look for it first thing in the morning. The field policeman seems satisfied and asks if we had stolen a bicycle sitting down below.

"A bicycle!" says the first lieutenant. "What good would a bicycle do us four?"

That makes sense. The field police leave and we try to get back to sleep.

In the early dawn, we make our way to the anti-aircraft battery in Neukölln. We find it and report to the head of the battery. The four 8.8 cm artillery pieces are located on a railway embankment and behind them is a large building. As it turns out, it was a mosaic factory. The roof is gone, but the rafters and roof supports are still there. A few slate pieces hang from the little tower.

No one knows what to do with us. I get something to eat from the canteen. I am dog-tired and look for a place to sleep. Someone has dug

---

* *Malzkaffee*; also called *Ersatzkaffee* (substitute coffee). It contained a mixture of grains, and most often chicory (whose roots were baked and ground). It contained no caffeine.

** *Feldpolizei* – one of several terms for military police.

a hole in the railway embankment and covered it with a steel plate. I crouch in it. An older man appeared and explained that he had dug the foxhole within the safety of the railway embankment for himself and his family nearby. He went on to say that the Russians had crossed the Oder River and are now in front of the gates to Berlin. Before us, in the small, privately owned family garden plots, there are just a few workers left, badly outfitted with weapons, which they hardly know how to use. What's to be done?

I sleep, sleep, and sleep. One day? Two days? I don't know anymore. The rumbling of the front is very close. I crawl out of my hole. It is hectic and the battery is filled with general excitement. I report to the orderly room and am yelled at by an officer. Afterwards, I am sent to the little tower of the mosaic plant as an observer.

By climbing several ladders, I reach my observation post. So, there I sit; out in the open, in the air; on a board; with a telephone in front of me. I look to the East and see numerous bomb craters, fires and smoke columns. About one and a half miles away, there is a Russian stationary balloon that directs artillery fire. I report: "Strong tank sounds from sector three!" Pause. "Heavy fighting and tank sounds from direction 5!" (It must be noted that the entire horizon is divided into twelve sectors, like a clock.) "Russian fighters from direction 3," I shout into the telephone. They are coming closer and closer towards us, towards me. There is heavy firing. I put my head down under my steel helmet and close my eyes. I hear crashing, whistling and splintering. Oh God! A fighter turns and tries to return. Meanwhile, the quadruple anti-aircraft gun has come to life and is returning heavy fire, so that he turns away.

An ensign (officer cadet) comes climbing up the ladder. "Well, little guy, you're still alive. Were you scared?" I nod. He puts his hand on my shoulder and says, "I'll relieve you."

Reassured, I climb down, report to the *Spiess*[*], get a rifle and ammunition thrust into my hands, and at sixteen years of age, I am now an infantryman.

Suddenly, the howling starts, which keeps getting louder and louder. The first shells impact the small, privately-owned family garden plots, crashing, bursting, screaming; dirt and smoke rise up 100 to 130 feet. I think, *my God, if that hits us, it will be the end!* I wonder if any of the workers down there have survived.

"Stalin Organs[**]," someone says who is familiar with them.

---

[*] A nickname for the company sergeant, the highest-ranking non-commissioned officer in the company.

[**] *Stalinorgel*: German nickname for Soviet Katyusha rockets because the racks of rockets it shot looked somewhat like organ pipes.

The head of the battery gives the command, "Prepare to move the artillery!"

We are supposed to leave and take up a new position at the Tempelhof Airport Field. All of a sudden, we receive artillery fire on our position. Shells strike. There is crashing, splintering and howling. One anti-aircraft helper is hit in the jugular vein by a fragment. Blood squirts out of his artery almost six feet with each heartbeat. A medic runs to him, presses his thumb on the artery, and drags him into the cellar. One of our artillery units is back in operation in order to shoot down that dammed Russian stationary balloon that is directing the fire to our position. Our artillery keeps shooting, but doesn't hit it.

The head of the battery has us fall in. Volunteers are needed for attacking the already audible T34 tanks with infantry anti-tank weapons. He yells at us, curses, calls us cowards, but of course, does not step in himself. There are very few volunteers and they are mostly anti-aircraft helpers. I met one of them later while we were prisoners. He had actually blown up the first tank. My kindly corporal once told me, "My boy, never volunteer for anything; because if it goes bad, you will always have to say to yourself, it's your own fault. But, if you are ordered to do it, that's different. You have to do it."

It's night time and the tractors of the Berlin transport company have reached their destination with the artillery pieces in tow. Commands are given, and there is shouting and chaos. We are told to fill our knapsacks with sausage and canned goods from the kitchen. That sounds good to us. Who knows what is to come. "Whoever wants to, can throw their knapsack on one of the artillery pieces," someone shouts in the dark night. "I would rather throw away my rifle and my gas mask, than my knapsack," says the corporal, whom I had known from our days at the anti-aircraft artillery school. He was to be proven right. During the next few days, I survived from the provisions in my *rucksack**.

We depart. I'm walking next to the fourth artillery unit. Shells hit the ground all around us; there is machine gun fire as well as single shots. We move past tanks that have been partially buried and street-cars that stand at odd angles. We turn down one street and suddenly we are under very heavy fire from a Russian tank. They are approaching from the opposite direction. We run into the halls and cellars of neighboring houses. Finally, by way of backyards and gardens, we make our way to Tempelhof Airport.

---

*You should know that anti-aircraft soldiers do not call them *Tornister*, but *Rucksäcke*.

We rest for a short time and then meet in the underground rooms of the large reception halls. Murderous gunfire is taking place above us. We're a colorful lot, made up of sailors, pilots, infantry, anti-aircraft helpers and members of the labor service force, all tired and dirty. We haven't washed in days. Meanwhile, I have also lost track of the corporal. He was the last person known to me.

Someone arrives and gives everyone a bar of chocolate. I can't believe it! I'm looking forward to enjoying it and put it on the table to tie my shoe. I straighten up again and the chocolate is gone. Stolen! I'm devastated. How can you steal from someone when death is around the corner? There is icy silence. Everyone looks away. I am hungry and close to tears.

At Tempelhof Airport, Flak batteries fired directly on advancing Soviet tanks until the Germans were forced to withdraw on April 26th. On the same day, Hanna Reitsch* with Field Marshal Robert Ritter von Greim, flew in from Munich and landed on an improvised air strip in the Tiergarten to the West of the Reichstag.

By April 28th, the Germans were now reduced to a strip less than five kilometers wide and fifteen kilometers long: from Alexanderplatz in the east to Charlottenburg and the area around the Olympic Stadium in the west. That day saw the last serious attempt to break the Soviet encirclement of the city. General Walther Wenck, commander of the 12th Army attempted to break through the Soviet forces from the West**. Wenck's attack toward Berlin was aimed at providing the population and garrison of Berlin with an escape route to areas occupied by United States forces. By the same evening, after advancing about 24 kilometers, they were stopped still 32 kilometers short of Berlin, Wenck gave up the assault as hopeless and withdrew to the West, across the Elbe River where his army surrendered to the US 9th Army on May 7th.

During the evening of the 28th, von Greim and Reitsch flew out from Berlin in an Arado Ar 96 trainer. Fearing that Hitler was escaping in the plane, troops of the Soviet 3rd Shock Army, which was fighting its way through the Tiergarten from the north, tried to shoot the Arado down. The Soviet troops failed in their efforts and the plane took off successfully.

---

*Hanna Reitsch (1912 – 1979) was a world famous aviator (and even military test pilot) who set many female flying records and was known for her daring.

**The future German Foreign Minister, Hans-Dietrich Genscher, was among those in Wenck's army.

Early in the morning of April 30th, Battle for the Reichstag* began in earnest. The Soviets launched an infantry assault across the Königsplatz on the Reichstag. The Germans were well provisioned with food and ammunition and launched counter-attacks leading to close fighting throughout the night and the early morning of 1st May, when about 300 of the last German combatants surrendered. 200 defenders were dead and another 500 were already lying wounded in the basement**.

On April 30th Adolf Hitler committed suicide.

---

*Reichstag was the name for the German Imperial Assembly (congress or parliament) and is the name for the building that today houses the German Federal Assembly.

**See "Battle in Berlin" (http://en.wikipedia.org/wiki/Battle_in_Berlin).

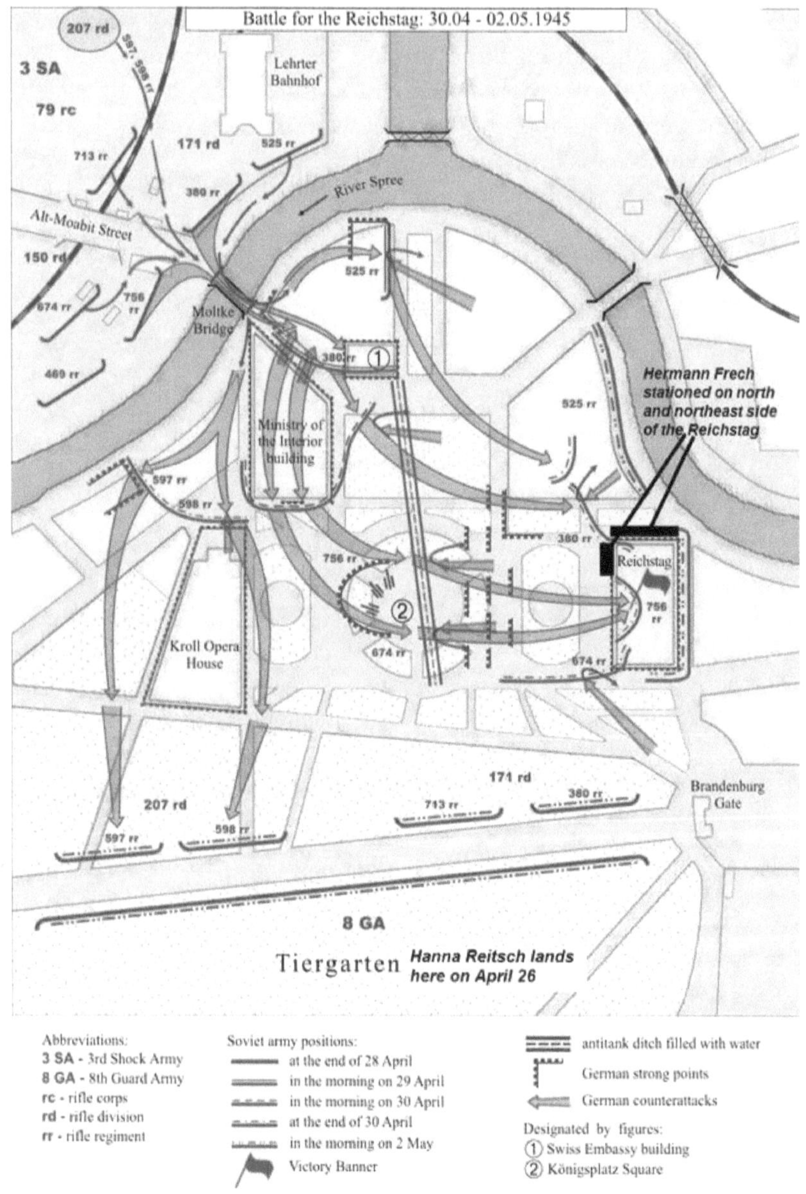

Source: http://commons.wikimedia.org/wiki/File:Battle_for_Reichstag_1945_map-eng.png

Chapter 5

Berlin – May 1945

In the assembly hall of the German Reichstag

At dusk, we're supposed to fight our way to the Reichstag. It is the end of April 1945. The night is warm. I sneak, run and storm after the others. At sixteen years of age, I am obviously one of the youngest. I don't know the way; don't even know where front, back, East or West is. There is shooting, crashing and fire everywhere. We reach the Reichstag, go past the guards behind doors with three-foot thick walls and enter the building. We find the entrance to the gigantic cellar vaults, collapse and sleep. A patrol wakes us up. In the dim light, we can see many wounded. We hear shouting down the hall.

"Who can still walk?" someone asks me. "Are you wounded?"

"No."

"Then go quickly up to the doors on the north side."

We take our time going up, past a group of *RAD–Mädchen*[*] and numerous wounded. Finally we are hunched down behind thick walls and peer over to the Landwehr Canal. The Russians have already reached the far side.

The constant crashing, shooting and explosions wear you down. Now we are told something different. A small troop is told to go over to the State Chancellery[**] and get hand grenades. We run out of the doors on the South side, in the direction of the Brandenburg Gate. The streets are filled with an uncountable number of dead, and in front of a fountain, they have even stacked one on top of the other. Senseless is what our troop leader also thinks, and he shouts, "Back." Not all make it back again to the thick walls of the German Reichstag.

Presently, I am behind the doors on the west side of the main

---

[*]RAD = *Reichsarbeitsdient* (Reich Labour Service): service was mandatory for all males (ages 18-24), and once the war began, for females. It was organized along military lines. *Mädchen* = girl(s).

[**]*Reichskanzlei* – this is the building where the German Chancellor had his offices. It was thus Hitler's headquarters.

entrance. An officer appears and says, "Tonight paratroopers will land on the East-West-Axis to reinforce us. Make sure you don't fire." We hear one or two Junker 52s. In the morning about 10 paratroopers have joined us. What a huge reinforcement! I admire their cleanliness and their beautiful uniforms and listen as they discuss their situation. A paratroop officer is bent over a map.

"That's where the Russians are. You go there, you over there and then we will have them in our pincers."

Oh my God, thinks the little anti-aircraft helper from Göcklingen, without ever having studied military strategy. *Do you have any idea of what you're doing?*

Except for the officer, I never saw any of the paratroopers alive again. A new order is given. A paratroop officer takes over the command. He assembles a troop of twelve men, including me. I get a better rifle. We are to storm out of the doors on the north side and go to the Landwehr Canal in order to prevent the Russians from crossing over. There is no time to think. One quick prayer, that's it! Everything seems to be happening in sort of a trance. Fear? Yes and no. Somehow, I feel protected as if I were in a large ball, which deflects everything. Very strange.

Reichstag Berlin, 2nd May 1945
Hermann Frech was positioned on the left and in front of the Reichstag.
(Photograph taken by a Russian soldier)

We are met with extremely heavy, murderous gunfire. The entire courtyard is full of grenade craters, shot-up streetcars, tanks and autos. There is shell impact upon shell impact. We jump from crater to crater. (Later, the crosses for zone refugees* who were shot will be found here.) I'm trying to jump out of a grenade crater. Raising myself up, I see something black streaking towards me. I throw myself down on the ground as the grenade explodes. Dirt flies over me, but I'm alive! If I hadn't experienced it myself, I wouldn't have believed it from someone else. I climb out of the grenade crater and into another one. There is already someone from our group in it. Thank God he is alive. He speaks with an East Prussian accent and says, "Boy, there is no point to this. We will not make it to the embankment."

After a while, during which we occasionally lift our heads, he says, "When the shooting dies down a bit, we'll run directly back to the Reichstag building." No sooner said than done. Three or four other troops follow us. The officer from before appears again and asks why we are here. I explain that we had lost visual contact with the head of the troop and were hardly able to peer out of the crater, because the gunfire was so intense. He yells at us, curses us, calls us dirt and names us cowards who had left their comrades in the lurch. So, here I am, a sixteen year-old boy, listening to this, and think, why didn't you come with us? This certainly appears to be a familiar phenomenon; we are always sent out, but the higher the military rank, the further back these gentlemen stay in their secure tracts of land. He is still raging, and who knows what he might have done to us if a messenger had not appeared to tell him that he is supposed to report to another location in the Reichstag immediately. As he's leaving he shouts, "I'll deal with you later". He is gone and is never seen again. We take our time getting to our position at the north doors of the Reichstag.

I'm wondering what date it is. Still April? Already May? No one knows. A lieutenant appears and says, "We have to hold out for only a few more days, Wenck's army is approaching and is about thirty-two kilometers (twenty miles) in front of Berlin. It will break the blockade and we'll be free!" Each one of us gets a chocolate bar. From experience, I finish it up right away. Together with a few others, I am sent to the main entrance at the West side of the Reichstag building. From there, you can see the zoological gardens**, can still recognize the East-West Axis, the shot-up trees, and further in the back, the tall zoological bunker still held by us.

---

*They are those who tried to escape over the Berlin Wall (beginning 1961).

**The famous *Tiergarten*

"Everyone, listen!" a voice says. "Tonight a Fieseler-Storch plane will land on the street to the Brandenburg Gate. It will be piloted by Hanna Reitsch. She wants to get the *Führer* Adolf Hitler out of here. Do not shoot under any circumstances! Understand?" We nod. Boy that would be something.

The Fieseler-Storch is a plane with two seats, which can fly quite slowly and requires a very short space for landing and takeoff. Because of the general noise of the battle for Berlin, I don't hear or see anything. Some said they saw something. As we know today, Hitler refused to leave the safety of the bunker in the German Chancellery. Only one general took the opportunity of getting out of Berlin, but certainly not without leaving a reminder for those remaining behind: to be brave to the last man, for the *Führer*, for the people and for the fatherland.

A Fieseler Fi 156 Storch

The command to stop shooting is lifted. A few others and I are sent to the east side. While crossing the inner courtyard, a shell explodes and knocks us to the ground. Dust and smoke fill the courtyard. We get up, but the person in front of me remains on the ground. He has such a beautiful, clean uniform: must not have been here long. "Hey, get up!" I call to him, He doesn't move. I bend over and take his hand. Dead. In my haste, I can't see any injury. Perhaps a small shell fragment has hit his heart. One second later and I would have been fatally hit in his place. I offer a short prayer of thanks.

We are told that the Russians are already on the roof of the Reichstag. Could be. It won't go on like this for very long. I hear that a small troop of officers and experienced soldiers want to break out tonight and fight their way to the West. Just don't become Russian prisoners! A few are said to have gotten drunk and then shot themselves. After hearing the constant propaganda about Russian imprisonment, we are all afraid.

The next morning there are no more officers to be seen. I pass by a field kitchen, stop, and look into a kettle. A miracle! It is half full of noodles and pieces of meat! No cook. No one can be seen. "Is someone here?" No answer. I grab a ladle and fill up a bowl. After also finding a spoon, I eat, eat and eat. When was the last time that I had eaten something warm? Not for weeks. The noodles are still warm and taste heavenly.

A young, stylish anti-aircraft soldier passes by. "Come with me," he says. "The Russians are upstairs, we'll waste them!"

"No," was my answer. In the first place I was bothered by the word "waste," and second, I remembered the saying of the first lieutenant: "Never volunteer."

Our numbers have dwindled a lot. Now there are only four of us lined up behind the thick walls of the western entrance gate. They start shelling it with artillery. How long will the walls hold out? And then?

It's clear to me: this is the end. It's done, finished. (Later, while I was a Russian prisoner, I met up with a soldier who was shooting at the gates of the Reichstag with artillery.) Now we are climbing into the subterranean caverns of the Reichstag that consist of an unimaginable number of halls and rooms. They are filled with wounded, and real close to us, pretty, but scared, *RAD-Mädchen*. We post ourselves behind the entrance door and guard it in shifts.

After Hitler's death, fighting continued through May 1st. Once Joseph Goebbels had committed suicide in turn, General Weidling met with the Soviet commander, Lieutenant-General Chuikov, on the morning of the 2nd of May and agreed to an unconditional surrender of the city of Berlin, and ordered the city's defenders to surrender to the Soviets. Most Germans, soldiers and civilians, were grateful to receive food issued at Red Army soup kitchens. The Soviets went house to house and rounded up anyone in a uniform including firemen and railway men, and marched them – approximately 180,000 men – eastwards as prisoners of war*.

*See "Battle in Berlin" (http://en.wikipedia.org/wiki/Battle_in_Berlin).

Is that a voice on the radio? I start looking around for it in the dimly lit room. There, not far from the door, probably to get the last bit of daylight is a radio operator. We listen… "This is the Greater German Radio Broadcasting Station, transmitting from Flensburg… While fighting for Berlin to the very end, the *Führer* has been killed." One hears the news and feels the seriousness of the hour; feels the cloak of history passing by. And the announcer goes on, "You will now hear a commentary about May 1st." Aha, May 1st! Finally, I have a date that I can hold onto. *When was the last time I washed myself? It has been so many weeks ago. I don't have anything clean to change into. When did I eat last? Thank God, I had noodles two days ago.* I find my way back to the field kitchen, but it is covered by stones and rubble. Luckily, there is some, although very little water left in the pipes. The commentator continues: "It doesn't look good for the Fatherland, particularly after the *Führer* suffered a hero's death. But, Germany was saved once before and experienced a better time after the catastrophe! And that will happen this time also." Those are the last words that I hear from the Greater German Broadcasting Station. A better time… A better time… I wonder. Will we survive to experience that? Where did the speaker get his optimism? Today we know he was right.

May 2nd, early in the morning: "Attention! Attention! This is the Committee for a Free Germany. Give yourselves up. Resistance is senseless. You will only endanger yourselves and your wounded comrades. The entire Reichstag is occupied," we hear through a megaphone. There is silence. What should we do? There is no officer to be seen; we have to make our own decision. The voice continues, "Don't be afraid. You will be treated well. But, if you don't come out by 10 o'clock, we will fill the cellar with gas." Silence. We look at each other and don't know what to do. We look for gas masks and find one. And what will happen to the wounded and to the *RAD-Mädchen?*

Someone says, "We're going up". We nod, throw away our rifles and hand grenades, and sneak upstairs. A German soldier meets us over the first stairway. He is wearing a black, white and red armband, and says that he is from the Committee for a Free Germany, and that we should go on up, that nothing will happen to us. We crawl over the rubble, up the second stairway, and are blinded by the bright light of the May sun. Then we see a few young Russian soldiers. They are laughing and have their machine pistols pointed at us. In their thin, light-brown uniforms and their radiant laughter, they don't appear to be unsympathetic. We are ordered to lift our hands high and then put them against a wall to be searched and frisked. We stand like that for a while, with our hands pressed against the wall. *Will we be shot anyway, the way we've always heard it in the propaganda?* In my thoughts there is time to say farewell to my father and mother, my dear grandparents, the love of my youth, and to Göcklingen. We wait. Why don't they shoot? We wait, wait and wait. Nothing happens.

Then one of the soldiers gestures that we should go with him. We climb over ruins, past the many dead and finally arrive in a room of the Reichstag, which is still partially intact. We are told to sit down. He offers us cigarettes, is friendly and says, "Hitler kaput, everything okay."

After a while he tells us to get up and we are brought to the assembly hall of the Reichstag. The hall is full of prisoners. There is just enough room for us in the same place where just a short time ago the *RAD-Mädchen* had been. They were gone, but their knapsacks are still lying around. Too bad! I grab a knapsack, throw out the women's laundry, but keep the sewing stuff, two towels, a few handkerchiefs, and an eating utensil.

There is a deafening explosion. A shell has landed in the opposite corner of the assembly hall. Most of the ceiling has collapsed. We are standing on the rubble and see blue sky above us. The wounded are screaming and calling. Someone says, "They have stomach wounds from the shrapnel and are done for." One Russian says, "Those are your comrades that are shooting mortars at us. Call them and let them know that you're Germans."

"Comrades, don't shoot! We're Germans!" is what came from hundreds of throats. Thank God there was only one shell explosion. The silence afterwards is completely strange to us. Everyone is in his own thoughts. We are told to leave the assembly hall. The wounded are left behind on the ground, whimpering.

Organized into three rows, we walk into town in a long line. Everywhere, the dead lie among destroyed houses. The smell of burning flesh fills the air. In one street, we pass by five half-tracks. They all appear to be fairly new, and have not been totally covered with camouflage. They probably met up with Russian flame-throwing tanks in the narrow streets. It's a terrible picture. All that is left of the upper portion of the bodies are black clumps, while the lower body parts with boots and green military trousers are still intact. The last half-tracks, which are open at the top, have open back doors, but the crews were not able to escape. Whoever ordered the use of open and thinly armored vehicles in a street fight must have been an idiot.

Dead German soldiers lay in bomb and artillery craters. Civilians and prisoners shovel dirt over them. Are they hiding the dead? I don't know; there are too many. Later they will become part of the missing.

It is the end of our walk. We end up at the Plötzensee Prison. After we pass the gate, we are directed to one of the buildings. We rest in the halls and cells and are soon overjoyed. There is water! Water! Clean water. With a little patience we can all drink our fill and later we can even wash our face and hands. And then sleep, sleep, and sleep. We sleep on the floor of the prison cells.

As always, the next morning we are greeted by a sunny, beautiful day in May! We fall in, this time in rows of ten, like in a parade, in blocks of one hundred men each. I am in the first block. The first five rows are made up of high-ranking officers: generals with red stripes on their trousers, colonels and majors. Only a few appear as if they had been in any military skirmishes, or show ordeals of the past weeks. The others wear uniforms that are well taken care of; beautiful boots made of fine leather and knapsacks filled to capacity as if they had been preparing to be prisoners for a long time. I am only two rows behind the officer's block, and have plenty of time to observe everything before we depart. Finally, we are off! The long line begins to move. From everywhere come new columns of soldier prisoners. Soon, everything becomes clear: they're making a propaganda film. We pass the Reichstag; walk through the Brandenburg Gate, along the street *Unter den Linden* and past the cathedral. There are film teams everywhere taking pictures. Civilians and other prisoners are still clearing the way, cleaning the streets and removing the rubble, so that we can continue walking. We are a wretched lot, just like the columns of Russian prisoners, who we saw in the weekly film revues in earlier times. It reminds me of a poem, which was once meant for Napoleon's soldiers, fleeing from Russia.

"Mit Mann und Ross und Wagen, hat sie der Herr geschlagen."
(Man and horse and wagon, the Lord beat them all.*)

In the evening, we return to the Plötzensee Prison, a tired lot. This time I end up in a machine hall, surrounded by pumps and generators.

*This is the beginning of a song composed by Ernst Ferdinand August in 1813 after Napoleon's disastrous retreat from Russia.

Next to me, sitting on the floor, are two middle-aged members of the military. They carry on a conversation and appear to know each other well. I'm taken aback. Is that not the dialect from the Alsace region? They talk to me and ask where I'm from. "I'm from a little village near Landau *in der Pfalz*[*]," I answer. They say that they are wine growers from a village near Schlettstadt in the Alsace region. We talk about vineyards, and how ripe the grapes probably already are during this extremely warm spring.

Finally, in a heavy Alsatian dialect they say, "Hermann, stay with us. As Frenchmen, we will probably be released early, and if we want to return to the Alsace region[**], we will have to pass through the Palatinate somehow. And then when the train slows down, we'll just jump off." I nod.

"Know anyone in *Elsass?*[***]"

"Sure," I answer, "Hartmann Ernst in Kronenburg, near Strassburg[****], at Oberhausbergerstrasse 20. He was in school with my father in Kronenburg and is a good friend of my fathers."

"Well, then you just say that I'm your uncle and you want to go there." For the first time in months I had the feeling that here are two people who have my well-being at heart. And in spite of the cold floor, I go to sleep peacefully.

---

[*]English: the Palatinate (a mostly forested region in Germany across the border from French Alsace.

[**]English / French: Sélestat

[***]Elsass is the German name for Alsace.

[****]English: Strasbourg (the largest city in Alsace)

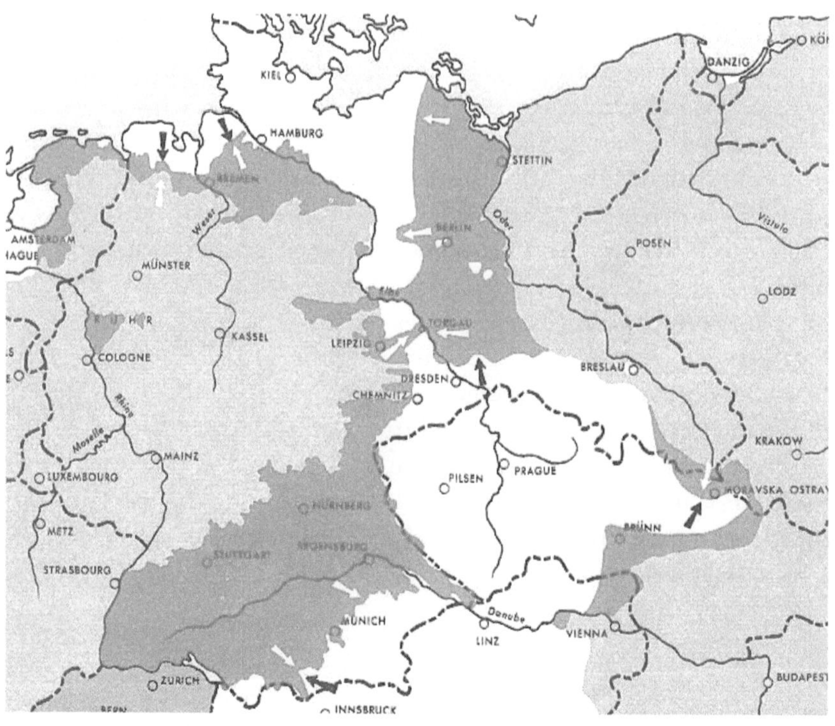

Germany: May 1st, 1945
Atlas of the World Battle Fronts in Semimonthly Phases to August 15th, 1945: Supplement to The Biennial report of the Chief of Staff of the United States Army July 1st, 1943 to June 30th, 1945. To the Secretary of War Army Map Service.
Public Domain: Work of US Army

White areas = under German control
Light gray areas = under Allied / Soviet control
Dark gray areas = areas of fighting

Chapter 6

Prisoner – May 1945

Hitler was dead and Germany had surrendered. On May 7th; representatives of the *Oberkommando der Wehrmacht* (German Armed Forces High Command) signed surrender documents in Rheims, France. On May 8th, another surrender document was signed in Berlin.

About two million German POWs were held in the Soviet Union during and after the end of the war.

The long walk to the East

We line up in three rows and walk through the prison gate. It's probably May 4th, 1945. I'm still sixteen years old, and what have I all experienced! My mother probably still thinks that I'm in good hands in the anti-aircraft school in the peaceful Bavarian Allgäu.

I stay close to those from Alsace. We travel on the *Reichsstrasse* 1*, which goes through Berlin, and leads east all the way to Königsberg in East Prussia. The suburbs look a little better, even with everything shot up at certain strategic points. Russian tank formations are still streaming into the city. My God, what great masses of T34 tanks there are! I gave up counting after a few hundred. How relieved we are whenever we would see three or four tanks on our side! There are trucks between the tanks, all of them American types. Seated on them are young Russian soldiers, shouting, "Hitler kaput!" They throw small things at us. Once, when the auto convoy comes to a halt, a few jump off and call out, "watches, no watches?" while they look at our wrists. Whoever has beautiful boots doesn't have them for long and will soon be walking in his socks. This affects mostly high-ranking officers. No one wants my shoes.

*National Highway 1 was the main East-West highway in northern Germany, and ran eastwards as far as Königsberg in East Prussia (Russian: Kaliningrad). It has not yet been replaced by an Autobahn.

The days in May, 1945, are hot. I get thirsty toward evening, very thirsty. But there is no water. We are part of a long column, which I would estimate to be about half a mile long. At dusk we are herded into an open field. Surrounded by guards and extremely tired, most of us soon fall asleep.

The cool of the morning wakes us up. We stand around and look for something to drink. In vain! When was the last time I had something to eat? Oh yes, the noodles in the Reichstag. In thinking back, they seem like they were the best tasting food that I had ever eaten. Silence again, walking, putting one foot in front of the other. Most of the streets are paved, and next to them is a sandy strip, which was meant for horseback riders in earlier times. We pass only a few inhabited villages. Now and then someone looks out of the window, half hidden, holding the hand in front of his mouth in astonishment. It's a damned hot day. I want to throw away my coat. "Hey, you'd better keep it. It's cold in Siberia; you'll be glad that you kept it."

Someone else says, "Think of last night, it got damned cold toward morning." In the evening, the usual: we camp in an open field.

We go on toward the Oder River. Toward midday it will be hot again. We go through a village and hear the first loud shouts: "Water! We want water!" No reaction from the guards. In the next village women have placed buckets of water at the side of the road. Today, I'm pretty close to the front and hope to get a swallow, but the Russians kick the buckets over. A few prisoners run over and try to lick the dirt, but are knocked back by the guards using their rifle butts.

The problem is not that it is the third day without food, you don't notice that. But the thirst! It drives everything else away. There is only one thought, water, water! My companions from Alsace try to comfort me. "Hermann," they say (how nice when you are called by your name!), "hold out. Maybe there will be something in the evening." And they go on to tell me how they became German prisoners in 1940 and didn't get anything to eat or drink during the first days. Of course, it wasn't as hot then. But where would a sufficient amount of bread for such masses of people come from in the middle of the war?

There. First Stop! Two railroad-crossing gates close in front of us and block our way. The front part of the column still got through. That means that we have to run hard to catch up to. I take advantage of our stopping and get the eating utensils from my knapsack, take the cover off the container and run back and forth in the ditch, in the possible hope of finding where the water enters the drain; the way I am accustomed to seeing it in Göcklingen. In vain! When I return to my place in line, my cooking utensils are gone. My God, that's not possible! I place the lid on my knapsack and go looking for them. Perhaps another "comrade" was also looking for water. A long freight train passes. I have to return to my spot. Now they have stolen the lid to my cooking utensils! I'm close to tears and ask myself how much more I will still have to give up to pay for all my inexperience. "*Davai! Davai!*"* shout the guards. We have to find the column in front of us.

The mid-day sun is burning hot, I can hardly move on. My vision is getting dim. "You have to hold out, little guy. Pull yourself together! Do you think that if you sit down, there will be a cart at the end of the column to pick you up? I don't see one. They'll just shoot you down and then you'll lie in the ditch! Get up, pull yourself together. Hold out!" Such words ring in my ears. But I can't, I am so terribly thirsty! I think of my mother, my grandparents and start to pray, *Lord, don't let me die here! Help me, Lord Jesus!* I pray several times, fearfully, desperately. Now, you can believe it or not, you can believe whatever you want. But, all my burdens were suddenly lifted. I felt as if someone was helping me up, as if I was being carried. I am literally floating. Yes, "floating" seems to be the best description. And then I make another quick prayer to the heavens.

I hold out until evening. Now, of course one can say that your adrenaline level was so high that your body gathered the last bits of energy. It could be. But for me, this experience was a wonderful thing and a turning point in my life.

What could still possibly happen to me?

In the evening, the usual: overnight in an open field. How many miles have we walked already? We estimate and agree on about thirty-five miles. Then we should be able to reach the Oder River by tomorrow. While it's getting darker, we run across the open field, looking for a low area, where we can lie down and go to sleep. What luck! There are two rows of turnips. We break a few apart using our shoes and eat the pieces. What tastes better, turnip pulp or the water that's in them? We try to suck out the water by chewing. What a delight!

May 8th, 1945. Early in the morning we are on the march. Within a few miles we reach the Heights of Seelow, a slight rise at the edge of the Oderbruch** region. This is where the last big battle took place on

---

*Russian: "Go!" or "Hurry up!"

**The *Oderbruch* is a low-lying region along the Oder River where the river splits into many courses before reuniting on its way north to the Baltic Sea.

German soil. Tens of thousands of Russians and Germans lost their lives here. It was the final defensive battle before Berlin. While the street gradually leads down to a ravine, I have time to look around. I've never seen anything like this! The countryside is covered with countless demolished tanks, trucks and artillery pieces. It's unimaginable. We approach the Oder River. The following picture is riveted in my mind: a German tiger tank, one of the largest and most powerful tanks in existence had attempted to use the relatively narrow causeway to reach the top of the Oder dike. Due to its heavy weight, the sides of the causeway collapsed and it came to rest on its bottom plate. Nothing went anymore. The treads turned in the air and had no contact with the ground while the cannon pointed skyward, almost like our anti-aircraft guns. Other than that, it appeared to be completely intact. Why would anyone shoot at it since it had taken itself out of action?

We reach the bridge of the Oder River; a pontoon bridge, guarded by Russian soldiers. A few prisoners think about jumping into the river, hiding under the bridge and then swimming to shore at night. But they give up this thought since the river is guarded too well, and aside from that, it is daylight. We march through Küstrin. This former Prussian fortification on the east side of the river is almost totally destroyed. We reach the plateau of the fortification, which is in relatively good shape. A number of buildings and barracks are clustered around the large inner courtyard. Apparently it was once a prisoner of war camp for Russian prisoners. We are told that we will be staying here for three days and are allowed to move about freely within the camp. I again meet up with the two from Alsace and they take me back to their barracks. "Hermann" they say, "you stay with us." Someone who'd acquired a tri-colored flag hangs it on the barracks.

During the night there is a lot of shooting, almost like New Year's Eve. We are not able to sleep and in spite of being very tired we step out in front of the Barracks. What's going on?

"The war is over! The war is over! Germany has capitulated!" Sounds of jubilation erupt from the Alsace barracks. Questions come up in my mind: will I ever get home again? What happened to my parents? Is my father still alive or did he die like Uncle Ludwig? What will become of Germany? Will it be divided into little pieces, the way it was described in the newspaper once? But there is water, water, as much as you want to drink! What a delight! Now I notice that I am hungry again.

May 9th, 1945. A Sunday filled with sunshine! Someone said that there was still a person in the barracks from Kronenburg. They call him, but of course, he doesn't know me, nor unfortunately Hartmann Ernst either. Later we are supposed to go out and do some exercises. The commands are given in French. German countrymen stand around and wonder what is going on. I also ask myself, what's this nonsense all about? After some time when the whole thing is over, I get my bundle, take my leave from my Alsace friends and go back to the barracks occupied by Germans.

At noon there is supposed to be food. But I don't have a container in order to get the soup! I go anyway. I stand in line and wait. Another prisoner comes up to me. I had seen him with those from the Alsace group. He said that he was not from Alsace, that he had only lived in Strasburg with his parents during the war. He lends me his eating utensils and I get in line in the back. It's almost my turn, but then we are told, that's all. Finished. There is no more soup! The soup consisted of a handful of wheat grain, with some salt cooked in water. It was to become our daily meal for the next months. Still, we get a crust of fresh, wet bread. I finish it, crumb after crumb. Since that time, I can't stand bread going to waste.

We fall in to get our haircut. A German "camp policeman" tells us that we'll have to get our hair cut immediately in order to be recognized easier as prisoners. We have to sit on a wooden bench facing each other and then get a pair of scissors (a dangerous weapon!) and, under supervision, have to cut each other's hair. We really look terrible afterwards. Luckily we don't have a mirror and are only able to see the messed-up hair of others. Later our hair is cut with a machine, so it is more even and looks a bit better.

May 9th, 1945. Today is my birthday. I have turned seventeen, am homesick and crawl into a corner. I want to be alone. I am thankful that we don't have to march on the street today, that I am not thirsty, that I can wash myself and in particular wash my feet. When was the last time that I changed my clothes? I try to remember; it must be months ago.

It is late in the afternoon. We are all supposed to assemble in the large inner courtyard and then seat ourselves in a square configuration. We wait. We're used to that. A troop approaches with six two-wheeled carts. Tar barrels hang between the wheels, filled with liquid manure from the toilets. Earlier in the morning, prisoners had been ordered to fill the tar barrels with the manure using tin cans. Commands are shouted, but I don't understand them. The men start moving, pulling and shoving the carts, always in a circle. They are all wearing brown-yellow party uniforms. I find that strange. The Russians think that they are high party functionaries that they had captured in Berlin. What a mistake! As it turned out later, they are small fry from the *Volkssturm*[*], the last recruits, mostly in the age between fifty-five and sixty-eight. Apparently, there were still many party uniforms in Berlin and these uniforms were given to the recruits. The Russians erroneously view these people as high party bigwigs. In reality, they are simple workers, employees and some even opponents of National Socialism. They are the ones who have to pull the manure carts around in front of us. At a given command, they are supposed to start singing. First they sing the German anthem, and after that, "*Die Fahne hoch*[**]" (The Flag on High), the sound ringing out in the courtyard. At first they sing loudly, but then softer and softer. It is hot and the old men can hardly go on. "*Bistriey! Bistriey!*" (Faster, faster) shout the Russians. We are supposed to clap to show our approval. No one is clapping. Who came up with this idea on the first day of peace? Perhaps the Russians experienced something similar in a German prisoner of war camp?

---

[*] "People's Storm": semi-military defense force, made up mostly of boys and older men.
[**] Also known as the *Horst Wessel Lied*. It was the Nazi Party anthem.

Chapter 7

Prisoner of War Camp – May/June 1945

Damned or Providence of God?

May 10th, 1945. Again we have a warm, beautiful spring day. We continue walking east on *Reichsstrasse* 1, in the direction of Posen*. The villages that we now pass are totally deserted. The Germans have been driven out or have fled and there are no Polish here yet. We walk through the Warthegau region. The trees and shrubs are filled with soft, lush leaves. The fields are unplowed, sometimes dug up for trenches and covered with shell holes. I think about my having turned seventeen today, but continue walking, always walking to the East. I wonder: are my parents or my grandparents thinking about me? Of course they are. How much they would have liked to bake me a cake. But I would prefer a glass of water. It has gotten hot again this afternoon. We've already marched more than twelve miles. We read the name "Landsberg an der Warthe**" on a sign. We will not make it to Posen before it gets dark. Landsberg is relatively unharmed and eerily empty. We walk up a long inclining path and then we see a collection of beautiful buildings in a park. I am reminded of our clinic in the *Pfalz*. As we found out later, it was indeed a former psychiatric institute. Across from it, there is an immense prison camp; probably a former German camp. Two approximately nine foot high double fences, crowned at the top with four rows of barbed wire enclose the camp. We enter through a double entrance gate, guarded with towers. The approximately eight hundred prisoners are apparently not a problem. Each one hundred is assigned to one barracks. Inside, they are filled with two sets of bare boards, one over the other, reaching from one end of the barracks to the other on which we are to sleep.

*Polish Poznań, the city had been part of the German Empire until the end of WWI and reincorporated into Germany 1933-45. Posen is located in western Poland.
**Modern day Gorzów Wielkopolski (Polish)

We are still supposed to get something to eat. We are called up and stand in line. I stand next to the line, hoping that someone will lend me their eating utensils. I'm in luck and receive a bowl of weak soup, which I finish with delight, more because of the liquid than its content. It is still light outside. I wander around the kitchen barracks, find a pile of garbage, which I try to separate with my shoes and discover an empty, slightly rusty tin can. What a treasure! I clean it with sand and grass and am overjoyed that I now have something to get a little soup with, if there is some. Thinking it was a good day; I go to the barracks, lay my coat on the hard boards, put the knapsack with my few belongings under my head and try to go to sleep. There is very little room. We are only about twenty inches apart from the next person. I think about home, pray an evening prayer from the church songbook and fall asleep. It doesn't take too long though, before I start scratching here and there. Others are also turning over, slap, moan and curse. Someone says, "Wanzen." *Wanzen?** I'm only familiar with something that sounds like that, with which we used to attach posters to the gates. No, these are hungry, little, flat, red bugs, a quarter to almost half an inch long, which live in the cracks of the ceiling in the barracks and at night fall down on us. No, this was not a restful night. I am glad when it starts getting light. Here and there one can still see the bugs filled with blood as they quickly scurry back into their hiding places. Disgusting.

"Get up!" someone shouts into the barracks. We go out, line up and get ready to march. Again. There is no opportunity to wash nor is there even a swallow of water available. As always, we line up in a group of one hundred, are counted and counted again. Correct, there are one hundred of us. But the large column is not moving yet. We have another hot day ahead of us and I am already thirsty! I lay my bundle on the ground, grab my tin and try to find some water somewhere in the camp. I look into the rain barrel. It's empty. I run here, run there; nothing. Quickly I run back to our group. To my dismay, it has already left and the whole place is deserted. Only my bundle remains alone in the dusty area. I pick it up, look helplessly around and become frightened. We have all heard the most terrifying tales of what happens to those who don't behave properly.

Another prisoner is quickly running towards me. I can tell from his green armband that he is a member of the camp police. "You damned dog, you bastard!" he shouts at me from afar. "I'd like nothing better

---

**Wanzen* is a German term for thumbtacks and bedbugs (and for "bugs," the type used as a listening device).

than to beat you to a pulp, you damned dirty swine!" I'm standing in a large open area and don't know what to say. He leaves.

After a while, another camp policeman comes, and just says, "Come with me!" Cautiously I ask him whether I will be locked up or sent to catch up with the others. "Keep your trap shut, you dog," is the answer. He leads me to a smaller barracks with the sign LAGERPOLIZEI* on it. I sit there and think, *Hermann, what have you done?* Even though there is a water can on the table, I don't dare ask for water.

"Let's go, come along," someone hisses at me. I want to grab my knapsack. "You can just leave that here," he says. Oh no, will I now also lose my last few belongings as well as my tin? We run through the camp to the fence. Am I to be shot? As a prisoner, one becomes a thing, at best a number. But, a human being? Shot while attempting to escape it will say in a brief report, and the matter will be closed. But it didn't end that way.

When we arrive at a little gate in the fence, I get a rake and a green armband. "You are now a member of the camp police," says the chief of this group. He signals the guard in the tower, opens the door and we enter the area between the two high fences. The gate is locked, and the chief leaves. The three of us are now between the fences and start to rake the ground, leaving parallel lines.

"Why are we doing this?" I ask.

"They want to be able to see the tracks of escaped prisoners," the oldest of the two responds. He also says that his name is Georg Böhm and that he is from Karlsbad in the Sudetenland. While there, he had also been with the police. Soon, he becomes my friend, almost in a fatherly way. He then tells me why the chief had been so angry with me. Since I was unaccounted for, the Russian police force that guarded the column had grabbed one of the camp policemen, and while I am raking here, he is the one who is now walking in the direction of Posen instead of me.

After a few days, the constant replenishment of soldier prisoners from the area of Berlin subsides. Because of my work, I soon have an overview of the situation. Even though hundreds continue to leave for the East every day, there are still more than a thousand prisoners in the camp.

Sometimes, we get a little extra bread. I try to dry out a fist-size chunk of bread on a board above me. The wet bread constantly makes

---

*Camp Police

my stomach growl and gives me gas. The next morning I get a terrible surprise. During the night, bed bugs crawled into the hollow areas of the bread. Not suspecting anything, as hungry as I am, I take a big bite and immediately spit it all out. Yuck, yuck, yuck. I've never had anything so nasty in my mouth, not even close. Terrible! Now I can understand why no bird or animal eats these bugs. In any case, Böhm sees to it that I can move to a smaller, bug-free, camp police barracks.

Today is my lucky day. While raking, I find a nail that I put in my pocket. In the evening I use a rock to hammer two holes into my tin and make a handle out of a few pieces of wire. Finally I have an eating utensil that is useable, but I still have to drink the soup since I don't have a spoon. I go about gathering some dandelion leaves for the vitamins. I tear them up into small pieces and put them into the weak soup to give it a little taste.

Tomorrow, most of the prisoners will move into the modern-looking Agfa Works factory, located between Landsberg and Posen. All the machines will be disassembled, loaded on freight cars and shipped to Russia. When the Polish return, they will find only empty halls with nothing in them.

At some point it is also our turn, but we merely have to sweep out the already emptied halls with birch brooms. On the way back, we pass by some open railroad carriages. I look inside and see something white. I turn and step closer; a man is lying there; an old man with snow-white hair. These railroad carriages probably brought Germans from East or West Prussia to the East Zone. Since those in the carriages had to get out quickly (we're only too familiar with the Russian "*davai, davai*" [hurry up, hurry up]), the old man remained lying on the floor of the freight car, since he couldn't walk. He's probably been lying in this freight car for days now and would have continued lying there, until the train is loaded and leaves for the East. This would surely have meant his death.

Arriving back at camp, I quickly look up the German camp commander and tell him what I have seen. He promises that he will look into the matter. He's a good guy, from Heilbronn, who always steps in for the prisoners whenever he can. I meet him again the next evening, and he tells me that the Russians had picked the old man up yesterday and brought him to the military hospital. He is still alive. "Thank you," I say to him; and I thank God that there are still people with compassion.

Meanwhile, it is June. The sun beats down on us without mercy. But we have water enough to drink and also enough for us to wash ourselves, except for the sweaty and bad smelling clothes! I wash my socks and underwear in cold water, without soap and somehow they smell a bit fresher. Often, I wander through the camp, hoping to meet some acquaintance or other; I can do that with my green armband. Only the officer's camp, in which several hundred officers are locked up, is off-limits to me. But I can talk with them at the fence. They are so bored and envious of anyone who is allowed to work. One of them told me that they had started a choir, directed by a famous conductor. A Protestant priest is also partially reciting *Faust*, Part I, by memory, and then they discuss it afterwards.

I wander through an empty barracks, and of all things, a thin, striped pair of civilian pants is lying on a guard bed. There is no one any longer there to whom they could belong. Happy with my new treasure, I run back to our barracks. With a razorblade, I cut off the pant legs a hand-width below the knee, get the sewing stuff, which I still have from the *RAD-Mädchen* at the Reichstag building, turn over the cloth that is hanging below my knees and sew it together. Any woman would have been horrified at my terrible job, but it holds up and I'm now wearing shorts during the hot summer days.

I have a conversation with a tank soldier today; he can easily be spotted by his black uniform. He asks me where I'm from, and I answer from the Palatinate. "Oh, from the *Pfalz*," he says, "I was there at Christmas time. We were called up with our tiger tanks, since the Americans had already advanced past Weissenburg[*] into the *Westwall*[**] region. We were able to push them back to Hagenau. But then the Russians advanced to the Oder River, and we were quickly transported there by train." He then proceeded to tell me about the terrible tank battle at the Oderbruch and how many Russian tanks they had destroyed. However, new ones kept coming, always more. Their superiority was indescribable. Finally, they ran out of fuel and ammunition. He was one of the few survivors; at least he never saw anyone from his unit again. I asked him if all the villages near Weissenburg were destroyed. "No," he said. "When we left, only the villages in Alsace, between Hagenau and Weissenburg were heavily damaged, but hardly any on the Palatinate side. I began to hope for the possibility that our house, or that of both of my grandparents, might still be standing.

---

[*] French: Wissembourg, a town on the border with Alsace.

[**] The *Westwall* was named the Siegfried Line by the western allies. It was a fortified line along Germany's frontier with France, Luxemburg, Belgium and the Netherlands. Remains of it can still be seen.

Every month, all prisoners are examined. For hours we stand around, naked, before we are examined by a Russian female doctor and a German male doctor. We have to bend over, turn, and are then categorized. In May, I was a level two, which means that I am qualified for all types of work, but not the coalmines. In June, I get to level three: good for normal work. In September, I am categorized to a level four: only light work. In October, I'm told that I have "dystrophy" due to faulty nutrition. I am not able to work at all. Some have very bad health problems. I remember one person, who had a scrotal hernia, which hung down to his knees, and someone else, who had a protruding hernia of the groin.

Hundreds of us are standing in line along the fence leading to the *Reichsstrasse.* We are examined again. Each time, a few are picked out and transported off to Siberia. A refugee procession passes by the camp fence. There are old women with backpacks, mothers holding children by their hands and baby carriages loaded to the top. Because they are unable to walk any more, white-haired old men and women sit in children's wagons, pulled by children or women. This pitiful procession seems endless. Suddenly, there is an outcry. A prisoner has recognized his family. He calls to them and asks about various persons. They block the procession and slow it down. "Why is our," (I have forgotten the name of the girl) "sitting in the baby carriage? She's no baby and can walk," asks the man. The members of the family stop and step aside, so that the others can pass by.

"She is blind," a family member responds.

"How?" the man wants to know. But the family is back in line; they don't want to be left behind alone. He tries to run with them a bit along the fence. I can't understand the answer. The man turns and begins to cry and weep. He is not ashamed of his tears.

We are very fearful of dysentery. Whoever gets it is lost, is thrown on a cart and taken away. I'm constantly on the lookout for charred pieces of burnt wood. Finally, my chemistry class in school is paying off! Once, I also got diarrhea. I then chewed on the remains of the collected charcoal pieces as much as I could. To my amazement, it helped. Again, a quick prayer of thanks to Heaven.

This morning a young Russian picks me up. I ask myself: *What's this all about?* We walk out of the camp, down the road, over to the former clinic. He leads me to the old festivities hall, which I'm supposed to sweep out. There is a large, red painting on the wall. It represents the USSR. What a huge picture! Little Germany is next to it like an insignificant add-on. I ask myself, did Hitler never look at a map, or hear of Napoleon's experience?

I am summoned to wash dishes and mop up the kitchen. Four or five Russians are sitting nearby, drinking vodka from water glasses. They also let me have some. *Brrrr.* I cough and make a face. They all laugh. One asks me in good German, "What did you do at home?"

I answer, "I was a student.*" Hardly do I utter the words, when I think to myself, *Why did you say such nonsense?* I would like to be a student one day. It's too late.

He asks what I studied. I look around, and don't know what to say, so he finally says, "You're lying, go back to the kitchen." I'm ashamed and leave with a red face. But it's a good day anyway.

There are all kinds of leftovers lying around in the kitchen: a little bread here, the remains of a sausage there, ham and cheese. I eat a little of everything, always careful, keeping one eye open to make sure no one will catch me. After I finish, I get courageous. I throw a cucumber (for the vitamins) and a kitchen knife into some dirty dishwater. With this dirty water and its contents in a bucket, I walk past the Russians, who are meanwhile feeling the effects of the vodka, and are in good spirits. Behind a corner of a house, I first retrieve the knife and then the cucumber, wash them thoroughly under a water spigot on the outside wall, and finally hide them in my pant legs. What luck, that I am wearing my long pants today, but after all, it is already almost the end of September.

I tell the Russians that I am finished. One Russian checks everything and then says "*charaszo*" (good). The German-speaking, young student tells me to go over to the camp. I can't believe my ears. "Alone?" I ask. "Yes, take off," he responded. Cautiously I make my way back, looking around once more before I leave.

What's this? In the middle of some dirty water coming from a small waterspout, there is a grape! A grape! Sure, it's the end of September and spring and summer were hot. Perhaps they're also gathering grapes at home, if they're still alive. Okay, so we haven't heard from each other for three quarters of a year. My mother presumes that I'm probably still in the beautiful Allgäu region, or in the worst case, in an American prisoner of war camp.

I can't resist. I get the grape from the dirty water, sneak back to the spigot on the park side of the house and wash it over and over again,

*This was dishonest, as the German word Student refers only to university students. A grade school attendee is called Schüler ("pupil").

since I'm afraid of getting some disease from the dirty water. Slowly, very slowly I meander back to the camp, and eat the grape, which is not exactly sweet. Never again in my life did I ever eat a grape, which tasted so good. Thank God for this tasty delight! I enjoy the freedom of walking back without a guard. The camp guards watch me in surprise, as I just walk along without an escort. But since I'm going in and not out, they open the gate.

These body lice are terrible! They are big, much larger than head lice, which I still remember from kindergarten. They hide in the folds of your clothes and then come out to suck up their fill. Sometimes you scratch here, sometimes there. The whole thing is very unpleasant. Finally, delousing! Twenty men enter the delousing barracks at a time, undress and hang their rags on a wire coat hanger. The clothes are hung in a walled-in chamber and heated to about one hundred and seventy-five degrees Fahrenheit. Meanwhile, we fetch some water with wooden buckets and wash ourselves. After an hour, we get our still very warm clothes back, not smelling good, but nevertheless free of lice.

Chapter 8

Prisoner of War Camp – June/December 1945

Christ or communist?

"Hey, come with me." a prisoner says to me. "If you go to communist school in the afternoons, you don't have to work." No sooner said than done. So here we sit in a portion of the barracks that's been made into a classroom, wait and drink weak tea. Finally the commissar enters, but as we soon find out, he is not Russian by birth, but a German communist who fled to the USSR in 1933. He presents us with a picture of the world as I have never heard it presented before. Everything is in strong contrast to my previous beliefs. Whatever was white before is now black and vice versa.

The following afternoon, we go back. Attendance has thinned. There is a large white poster on a side wall, which has a quote from Stalin, "The Hitlers come and go, but the German people will endure forever!"

We are allowed to ask questions. Someone wants to know, when we might be going home. "You all know what damage the Germans have done in Russia and what crimes they have committed. You'll be released when Russia is rebuilt" is the answer. There is silence.

Another question, "And when do you think that might be?"

"In about thirty years." There is more silence, or was there a quiet moan? There are no more questions. Everyone is calculating. Depressed, we slowly walk out.

"You're lucky, little guy," says an older prisoner to me on our way back to our barracks. "When you get home, you'll only be forty-seven years old. You'll still have time to start over; but us? We'll all be retired pensioners, if we even live that long."

We're all depressed. Thirty years! That's a long time. Dejected, we saunter back to our barracks. I lie on the hard boards, but can't fall asleep. I wonder if Uncle Edward can perhaps help me out. He's in the American Diplomatic Service and America is an ally of Russia. But, how will he know where I am? Well, thirty years is a long time, and perhaps they'll look for me at some point.

Is it true? There is supposed to be a church service at a large assembly place in the middle of the camp. It is true. The Jewish camp commander, who always has an immaculate appearance and proper uniform, has authorized it. They come from all parts of the camp, many, hundreds. Even the officer camp is opened. Only the prisoners in the low cellars under the guard barracks remain locked out. You can see them through the iron gate. One cannot stand upright in the low cellars. They are supposedly members of the SS, or members of the army whose division committed pretty atrocious acts in Russia, or they stole something and got caught. When they are twelve in number, one hears that they disappear to work camps in Siberia.

So, here we stand in this large place in the middle of the camp. We are full of expectation. A Protestant priest begins: "In the name of the Father, of the Son, and of the Holy Ghost." The Catholics cross themselves. I don't remember what the epistle was about. The officer choir sings. The priest tells us not to give up hope, because there is peace. Japan has also capitulated after the dropping of two atomic bombs. God is with us, even here. We sing, "Great God, we praise Thee," and with particular heartfelt feeling, we sing the verse, "Lord, have pity on us." The plea travels to all parts of the camp. Frankly, some men have tears in their eyes. We all pray the "Lord's Prayer" in unison. A Catholic priest gives the blessing and finally we sing, "Now thank we all our God*." We give thanks from our hearts that there is peace, and find some solace in the second verse:

Der ewig reiche Gott woll uns in unserm Leben,
Ein immer fröhlich Herz und edlen Frieden geben,
Und uns in seiner Gnad erhalten fort und fort,
Und uns aus aller Not erlösen hier und dort.

(Oh may this bounteous God through all our life be near us,
And keep us in His grace, and guide us when perplexed;
With ever joyful hearts and blessèd peace to cheer us;
And free us from all ills, in this world and the next!)

---

*"Now thank we all our God" is a popular Christian hymn, originally composed in German (*Nun danket alle Gott*) circa 1636 by Martin Rinkart (1586-1649).

"It was beautiful," a prisoner from upper Bavaria says to me on the way back, "but when I think of the beautiful May services at home," and wipes the tears from his eyes, "I think we will stay true to our Christian faith after all!"

Good days, bad days

Today is a great day! When the cook saw that I, as one of the last ones to get my water soup, was drinking it from a tin, he asked me, "Don't you have a spoon?" I shook my head. "Here," he said and handed me a spoon made of wood. I am so happy and thank him from the bottom of my heart. To this day we still use this spoon. Of course, the colorful decorations as well as the clear coating over it has worn off long ago, but the spoon is just right for measuring portions from the bag of flour that we get from the miller. By the way, it is the only souvenir from my time as a prisoner.

Damn! Nothing to eat again! We miscalculated the time when we were raking between the fences and are too late for dinner. The kitchen is closed. Finished. Done. We sit around sad and hungry. I mention that I have been able to keep my watch, in spite of all the stealing. "You still have a watch?" They are astonished. "How did you do that?" I told them that in each camp before the inspection, I had dug a little hole with my shoe where I stashed my watch. The watchband had been removed a long time ago. I remembered the place where it was hidden and would leave it there until evening. When it was dark I would dig it up. From now on, we are never late for dinner again and I gained some stature.

But after a while, the chief of the camp police found out about it. He comes over to me and says, "You have a watch?" I nod. "Give it to me right now, or I'll report you to the Russians. You know what that means!" Owning a compass, a map or a watch is strictly prohibited. You can be assured of being arrested and sent to a special prison in Siberia.

Böhm, my fatherly friend from Karlsbad who had heard everything, said, "Hermann, give it to him!" I part with the watch with a heavy heart, since my grandmother had given it to me for my confirmation. After a while the chief comes back and brings me three slices of bread, and about eight tablespoons of sugar in a conical bag made of newspaper. What a wonderful dinner. How tasty!

The camp police chief had received a large bag containing a handful of *machiorka*, a dark and strong tobacco, which the Russians smoke after rolling it in newspaper to a type of cigarette*. This was apparently the point of the whole transaction. He is a heavy smoker and in the end, it was at my expense.

"*Wer kennt euch nicht, ihr kummervollen Nächte!*"
("Who does not know you, you sorrowful nights?")

Adapted from a poem by Johann Wolfgang von Goethe:

Wer nie sein Brot mit Tränen aß,	Who never wept to eat his bread,
wer nie die kummervollen	Who never sat through grievous hours
Nächte auf seinem Bette weinend saß,	Of night in tears upon his bed,
der kennt euch nicht, ihr himmlischen Mächte.	He knows you not, you higher powers.

October 1945. The nights have gotten quite cold, and the camp has meanwhile become pretty empty. All imprisoned officers are gone. Prisoners don't have to walk on foot any more. They are brought to the train station in Landsberg, loaded on freight trains and sent off to Siberia. The camp police have been disbanded. There is no more raking between the fences, and I have to move back to the big barracks. And once more I am plagued by the damned bed bugs!

It gets dark early now. I lie on the hard plank bed, covered only by my coat. My knapsack serves as my pillow. I get homesick. I know that my mother and my grandmother are praying for me. I can feel it; it empowers me and helps me. Do you know what it's like to be without a book, without a newspaper, or without having anything in writing for months? It's terrible! How thankful I am to each teacher, and each priest, who had me memorize poems or verses from a songbook. They are now spiritual nourishment to me and of immense value.

Again and again, I recite those verses and am happy when I am able to recite them to the end, even if it is a night later. "Command Me on Your Path," "Trust the Lord," "When it's Difficult for Us": what beautiful verses from the songbook! Or Schiller's "The Hostage," Rilke's "Lord, it is Time" or, "Autumn," "At Midnight" by Möricke, Goethe's "I wandered in the Woods by Myself," etc. What a valuable treasure. It gives me courage and keeps me alive!

*Machiorka (Nicotiana rustica), known in South America as mapacho, was smoked in Russia by the lower classes before normal tobacco became widely available (after WWII). It is a very potent variety of tobacco with a high concentration of nicotine in its leaves.

"Come with me," a Russian says to me and to four others who no longer have to work. We get into a small truck. In the bed of the truck there are pickaxes, baskets, sacks, a pail and an iron stand. We start driving and turn off the road onto a path. Being in the bed of the truck, we're pretty much shaken up. We drive through a forest area and finally end up near a field of potatoes.

"Get off," one of the Russians says, who actually speaks pretty good German. He tells us to take the picks and fill the baskets with potatoes. He then takes a staff, sticks it into the ground and says, "Dig to here." We can easily do that. The Russian goes back to the truck and rolls a *machiorka* cigarette for himself. We work slowly; there is no rush. These are good potatoes. I wonder where the Germans might be who planted them in the springtime. One of us goes to the truck and tells them that we are finished.

The other Russian gets out, takes the staff and places it some feet further away. We start to object. We don't understand. "*Nyet!* (No)" says the guard and disappears back in the truck. This time we work even slower. Finally the new portion is also done. We start packing up our stuff. After again saying "*Nyet!*" he brings an empty pail and tells us that we should also fill that one. We grumble. He then sets up a metal tripod, while the second one goes to the woods and starts gathering wood.

After a while, the Russian who remained behind indicates to us that the potatoes are for us and that we can eat them later. Now we don't have any problem digging up more potatoes! He goes to the truck cabin and fetches a canister of water. Meanwhile we have filled the pail with potatoes. He pours the water over them, goes back to the truck again and comes back with a bag of salt. The second Russian brings the wood. We help to chop it up into smaller pieces, while the other one spreads a handful of salt over the potatoes. Soon a fire is burning under the pail. We sit around the fire on the baskets and bags and wait for the potatoes to get soft. Then the Russian, who speaks pretty good German, tells us that he was a German prisoner with a family on a farm, who treated him very well, and that's why he wants to do something nice for us today. We're pleased and thankful to the German family on the farm. The potatoes are still not soft yet. The Russians go on to ask where we were captured; whether in Berlin or in the outskirts. One Russian wants to know where specifically. I answer, in the Reichstag. He responds that he had been shooting at the entrance gate with artillery. I told him that I was standing behind the entrance when it was being shelled. There is general amazement. He reaches his hand out to me and says that he is happy that we're still alive. It's hard to believe that these are simply coincidences.

Meanwhile, the potatoes are soft. We pour them out so that they can cool off faster and put some salt on them. What a delight! We eat all of them with the skin, since we don't have a knife. After we finish them and have eaten our fill, we pack everything together and load up the truck again. Before we leave, we see two people at the other end of the large field who apparently also want to dig up potatoes. The Russians say, "They're Polish," and shoot some bursts in their direction with their machine guns, but not with the intention of hitting them. It's evening when we return to the camp. For the first time I'm not hungry when I crawl on my bunk.

It's December. We have another examination. It's cold and uncomfortable to be standing around naked for a long period of time. Now it's my turn. Today, everything takes longer. The German doctor asks me if I was wounded, while pointing to a scar on my left knee. (I sustained the injury as a child when I tore my skin open on a nail. Since the wound was not clamped together, the scar can still be clearly seen today.) The doctor winks at me and tells the Russian female doctor in Russian that my knee had been wounded and that I can't stand or walk very long. He asks how old I am. I reply, seventeen. He translated that to the Russian doctor. She wants to know if I can prove it. I tell the German doctor that I have a paper in the sleeve of my coat, with which I wanted to apply, correction, had to apply, as an officer's candidate. Get the paper, he said. I told him that I was afraid it would work against me. "Don't worry," he said. "She doesn't speak German. It just has to have your date of birth on it." I get the paper and stand at the end of the line. I'm curious why there are only about fifty men being examined today. After it's my turn, the doctor takes my paper, unfolds it, and shows my date of birth to the Russian doctor. She writes something down. He gives the paper back to me and says, "You can go." Today I know that this was another one of those times of destiny in my life: she spared me from being transported to Siberia.

Chapter 9

December 1945

The trek back in ice, snow and other obstacles

This can't be true. Freezing cold, I wake up and look for my shoes. Nothing. Those able to work have already left. I run around the empty barracks in my socks that are full of holes, look here and there, nothing. Finally, back in a corner under the first bunk, there is a pair of shoes. I crawl through the dirt and dust, grab them and bring them out into the hallway. They are not mine! They are many sizes too large. I've never seen shoes this large before, but I have to wear them. To be running around in December with socks that have holes in them is not advisable. By the way, except for having a little diarrhea once, I was never sick! A prayer of thanks to Heaven! Since I don't have to work, I wander through the many barracks. In one of them, I find two metal taps, the kind we used to nail on the front of our shoes*. But where can I get nails? I keep looking. And indeed, I do find some small roofing nails in a little box. With the help of a rock and almost half-inch long nails, I nail the taps to the front of the soles from underneath. Of course, inside the shoes, the nails stick way out, but the shoes are so large, that I don't even come close to touching the nails with any of my toes. I try to walk through the camp with these giant shoes, always looking to see if I can't find a better pair. And would you believe it, one day I get lucky and find a good-looking shoe. I keep searching and also find the other one. They are really beautiful shoes! Do they fit? Well, sort of. They are really too small. But I don't want to believe that, and try them on without socks. However, it's already too cold for that. If I pull my toes back a little, they have to fit. They do, but for how long?

**Stosseisen*: metal forms nailed onto boot tips to protect them from wear.

When I have to go to the latrine at night, I notice that there is a full moon. The beautiful evening song by Claudius* comes to mind. I recite a verse to myself,

So legt euch denn, ihr Brüder,	In God's name, you brothers,
In Gottes Namen nieder;	Lay yourselves down,
Kalt ist der Abendhauch.	The evening air is cold,
Verschon uns, Gott! mit Strafen,	Spare us from punishment, God,
Und lass uns ruhig schlafen!	And let us sleep peacefully.
Und unsern kranken Nachbar auch!	And our sick neighbors too.

In half an hour, the moon will also be seen like this over Göcklingen. Please, take my greeting with you, to all who are important to me! Close to tears, I quietly make my way back through the coldness of the winter night to my hard and cold plank bed.

The next morning I have to move to another barracks. Why do I have to move again, I ask myself? Then I notice that only prisoners unfit for work are assembled here. Well, I'll find out what that's all about. Is it possible that, instead of walking, we might be driven to the East in trucks?

There's a lot of commotion the following night; noise of vehicles, the sound of boots on the pavement; commands; it's all very strange. I'll see what's going on in the morning. Let's sleep first. Christmas will be here soon. I recite an advent poem to myself, and fall asleep shivering.

Still half asleep, I hear someone shouting, "The Russians are gone!" What do you mean the Russians are gone? A few go outside, and come back to tell us, "The gate is wide open! There are no guards on the watchtowers anymore!"

I can't make any sense out of that, and go outside to see for myself. You can walk through the open gate to the street, and nothing happens! We go through the guard's barracks, a little apprehensive, but again, nothing happens. Everything appears as if the entire camp has been cleared. But why? Someone calls us to come over to the office: "Come here, there is something here!" And there really was something on the front of the desk. It is a riddle. Someone thought that it might be our release papers. We count the pieces, about the size of a post card, made of brown packing paper. Two words stand out in the

---

Das Abendlied, by the German poet Matthias Claudius.

middle. They are written in black ink and twice as large as normal text. Underneath are a signature and an ink stamp. But who can read Cyrillic writing? No one. The count of papers is fifty-two! Oh God, those are our release papers! Our faces show joy mixed with disbelief. Each person counts the number of letters in his name: Hermann – seven, Frech – five. I look for a brown piece of paper that corresponds to these numbers. I find it and hold my release papers in my hand. Wonder of wonders. I offer a prayer of thanks to Heaven!

But what shall we do? Someone says that we have to all stay together. He had heard that the Polish would hang any Germans they meet. Someone else says that he doesn't believe that; aside from that, most of the Germans are gone and there are hardly any Polish here. But we agree that, first, we should all stick together, and second, that we will not start trekking back to Berlin before dark on the former Reichsstrasse 1, which is a distance of about sixty miles.

We search the camp, looking for things that might be useful to us in our long trek. "Hey chum," says one to me, "why don't you go to the kitchen, there's a whole bunch of cooked horsemeat in a pot with broth that's still warm."

Quickly, I run over there. Meat; when was the last time that I've had meat? Way back in May, in the field kitchen of the Reichstag building, with noodles. But that was a long time ago. Knives lie around, there is salt in a pot and the valuable pages of a Russian newspaper, but there's no sign of bread. Have the others already cleaned everything out? I don't know. I cut off a large piece of horsemeat, wrap it in newspaper, then take a small handful of salt, also wrap it in newspaper, and finally, I wrap everything in more newspaper. I then cut off small pieces of meat, add a little salt, and eat them on the spot. It's almost like a type of pot roast. If only I had a piece of bread with it! But that's how we are: first we get something, and right away we want something else!

It has gotten dark. The middle of December is pretty cold. I don't have a cap or gloves. We march off. I have an apprehensive feeling, a mixture of hope, happiness and fear of the unknown. Off we go! The outline of the street is easily seen in the white snow. For the first few miles all of us are still together. I had chosen the tight shoes and gradually my feet start to hurt. I fall behind. I call to them in the front, but no one hears me, no one wants to hear me. I'm still paying for my inexperience, learning about comradeship and so on. We should all stay together.

I look back. The others have disappeared for some time. But there behind me is a straggler. I stop and wait. "It's nice that you waited for me," he says. "Stay with me so I won't be alone." He is also an anti-aircraft helper like me, but a little shorter and only sixteen. He's from Gross Gerau, south of Frankfurt. In Berlin, he knocked out a T34 tank with an infantry anti-tank weapon. I have the feeling that he doesn't feel good about it. He has problems with his shoes too.

We've been walking in the cold night for about four hours now, and the wind is blowing the powdered snow over the streets. Suddenly he says, "I can't go on any further!" My God! I tell him that we're on our way home, that he'll soon see his parents. He wants to lie down. At these temperatures that will certainly mean our death! But we drag ourselves on. After a while, we see the outlines of some houses. There is not a sound. Since we left, we have not seen one person or any vehicles. We approach one of the first houses.

"Hello, is anyone there?" I call out. No answer. I go to the front door. It is open. Once more, "Hello, is anyone home?" Again, no response. Carefully we open the door to the living room and enter. In the dim light we see several clothes closets, which were apparently brought here from other apartments. Other than that, the rooms are empty. Because we are cold and don't want to sleep on the floor, we tip one of the closets over, and lay down inside it. We take our ill-fitting shoes off our aching feet and put one of the shoes between the closet door and the jamb because we're afraid that we might suffocate. After warming each other up a bit, we finally fall asleep inside the closet.

It is late morning when we wake up. Who will get up first to check things out? Again, I call out. There is no sign of life. We put on our shoes and remain seated on the closet. We get our horse meat out, which of course is cold now, sprinkle a little salt on it and have breakfast. Has anyone ever eaten cold horse meat? You can believe me that no one needs to repeat this experiment! We tip the closet back up, close the doors and go out to the street. We have recuperated a bit, and it also has stopped snowing. Will we still be able to reach the Oder River today? A pine forest shields us a little from the wind. There, ahead of us, we hear the noise of an engine. Before we are able to jump into the woods, a vehicle appears from around a curve. In a magnificent American car, we spot a well-dressed American soldier and a dolled-up German girl. Both are very friendly, and ask us where we're from and where we're going. They tell us that there are no Polish here yet, and if there were any, they wouldn't bother us. "How far is it still to the Oder River?" I ask.

"If you start in the afternoon and walk all night, you can be there in the morning." In parting, they give us a pack of cigarettes and drive off, unfortunately in the other direction.

We walk on through the night. Now and then we stop and eat some snow to quench our thirst. Luckily, my companion is able to hold out. We tell each other what it will be like to get home, talk about food, washing and having clean clothes. We know that each step brings us closer to home. Home, home, home is what goes through my mind.

We reach the Oder Bridge in the morning, which has meanwhile become the outer boundary of Poland* and go to the border check-point, which is manned by Russian soldiers. We show our slips of paper, and a soldier takes them with him and leaves. After a while, he returns and indicates for us to follow him. Oh, not again! Our hopes drop down to zero. Does that mean that our release papers are not the proper ones? Questions, questions, while Germany is already in full view across the river!

A pail and a cleaning rag are placed in our hands. We are taken to two rooms that we are supposed to clean thoroughly. Then two more rooms. Occasionally a Russian looks in to see that everything is in order. All the while we are dog-tired from having walked all night. But the hope of going home keeps us upright and renews our strength again and again. Okay, now we just have to clean the toilettes and then the kitchen. We then get a plate full of stew. What a wonderful aroma. What a pleasure. Can we leave now? Our baggage was taken from us. No, you still have to sweep the courtyard, and then you can go. We sweep the yard with a broom made of small birch branches. Meanwhile it is almost evening, and a guard appears, bringing our knapsacks and our obviously correct release papers. Tired, very tired we cross the Oder Bridge home to Germany.

But wait. Again we are stopped. This time by the German Auxiliary Police, dressed in black, who are supervised by Russian soldiers.

We are allowed to pass. We find a temporary barracks next to the destroyed train station, go in, sit on the floor and go to sleep. Toward morning it becomes cold. We go outside to a clear winter day. We are told that empty freight trains pass by here all the time on the way to

*The victorious allies redrew Germany's eastern frontier, putting it on the Oder River. As the land east of the River had been mostly populated by Germans who were then expelled, this region was rather deserted in December 1945.

Berlin, and that they slow down because of the pontoon bridge, so thatyou can easily jump on. We wait and wait. It is midday. I get into a conversation with a woman who is old enough to be my mother. She asks where I'm going. "To Berlin, but I don't know the shortest way there," I answer. She says that she knows the way well, but that she has a backpack filled with wheat and a bottle of beet syrup, which is so heavy that she won't be able to carry it to Berlin. Since no one seems to know when the next freight train will pass by, or if there even is one at all, I offer to carry her backpack if she will show me the way. It's a deal. I have already asked my companion if he wants to come along. He answers, no, that he can't. He's totally finished. We say good-bye, wish each other good luck and are sad about leaving one another.

First, the woman and I walk along the railway embankment, stepping from tie to tie. We look down into the Oderbruch* and over to the Heights of Seelow. She points to her destroyed village across the way and tells me that is where she is from, that she had picked up some wheat and beet syrup from her brother-in-law there. His house was one of the few that were still intact. Her husband was a town clerk there and that they had a beautiful house. Then he was killed in the war, as well as her only son, who was only a bit older than I am. She now lives in Berlin-Marienfeld, together with her widowed brother, a retired postal employee. That's where she wants to go. We stop around noon. She is carrying my light knapsack and I'm, carrying the heavy one. On the railway embankment we open her backpack, sit on the grass at the edge, and each one takes a handful of wheat from the backpack, which we slowly chew. I don't mention the horse meat, but get some more wheat. Then we proceed to the dessert. I break off two twigs, give one to her, and keep the other one. As I have found out earlier, the motherly woman's name is Mrs. Manthey. Then we dip one twig after the other into the jar of syrup and lick it off. It's so good! I would have continued licking, but she said that she has to save the rest for Berlin.

After having probably walked a little over fifteen miles, we reach a train station. There is actually a passenger train there. Someone says that it is going to Berlin. We run, and by barely managing to squeeze ourselves in, we are able to find standing room in the overcrowded aisle of the train. "And what do you think? Wasn't it a good idea to walk on the railway embankment?" I nod. We continue west on the train for the next twenty-five miles toward Berlin.

*The gorge through which the Oder river flows.

We arrive in Berlin at dusk. It is the middle of December and gets dark early. We get out of the train. "And what will you do now?" she asks me.

"I don't know."

"Listen, Hermann, I will tell my brother that you carried the backpack for me, and that it would have taken a lot longer to get home without you. Perhaps my brother will agree and let you sleep there."

We walk out past Mariendorf to Marienfeld. There is hardly any destruction in this area. Both parts of the city are located in the American sector. We arrive at Proellstrasse 20 and stand in front of a little settlement house built in the twenties. I have to wait outside until everything is settled, then I can enter. A man is sitting at a kitchen table and looks up at me. He does not appear to be exactly friendly. Mrs. Manthey introduces me. "Are you sure you don't have lice?" he asks in a disgruntled way.

I lie and say, "Yes."

After a warm glass of fruit tea, I'm allowed to wash myself with cold water while standing in the bathtub. Does that feel good! But then, I have to put on my dirty underwear again. Brrrr! I tell the old man about my past and then I'm allowed to go to bed. It's a bed with white sheets! My God, when was the last time I did that. I think back. Yes it was in the beginning of February in Schongau. Now it's almost Christmas.

The next morning, soon after I got up and had a last look at the white sheets, a fat bedbug crawled over the bed! Thank God that I killed it! After a cup of malt coffee and a slice of bread with beet syrup, Mrs. Manthey brings me to the French sector of Berlin, since the Palatinate is located in the French occupied sector of West Germany. We say good-bye; I promise to write her when I get home. Later we exchanged numerous letters, and soon, we only referred to Mrs. Manthey as Aunt Gertrud. We visited her several times in Berlin, and she visited us in the Palatinate region. In the beginning, as long as it was necessary, we sent food packages to Berlin, and she would send us a book or two in return.

I register with the French sector office in Berlin. Yes, everything is in order, but they have no means to send me home. I have to go back to the American sector. There, in a former barracks area, I meet many former prisoners who want to go to southern Germany, to the American or the French occupation zone.

To begin with, we travel through the Russian zone on a freight train. We all squat down on the floor of the dark freight cars. It's cold. A few hum a song and are softly joined by others. They sing old folksongs, which soothe our mental state. What secret powers these old folk melodies have! Soon, we feel more peaceful and in a better emotional state. The train stops somewhere in the state of Hessen. We are unloaded and get into open, American military trucks that are waiting for us. Squeezed in so tightly that we can't fall over, we drive through the sunny but cold wintry day on the Autobahn toward Frankfurt. Frozen through and through, but happy to be closer to home, we end up at a large American prisoner of war camp near Hanau. I walk around a bit and meet Otmar Meyer from Göcklingen, who was in the navy. He tells me that the food here is rather poor. However, he does have two packets of powdered pudding. We walk over to the kitchen and ask if they have a little milk. But they laugh at us and ask if we know where we are. I still have some salt in my knapsack. We dissolve the powder in some water, put in a little salt and add our daily portion of watery soup to it. We are terribly hungry and together with a slice of white bread, we're able to manage our hunger somewhat. However, in no way is this recipe to be recommended.

Later, we are told to line up for an interrogation. In an anteroom we are told that we have to give up all, yes, all written documents, which we received as Russian prisoners. If we don't, we can count on severe punishment. I hand over my brown Russian release document. I ask if we also have to hand over the addresses of our fellow prisoners. Yes, those also. In short: everything. With a heavy heart I part with the addresses; also included are those of my two friends from Alsace. I was just too afraid.

I'm standing in front of the door to the interrogation room. They're just finishing up with someone inside. I hear someone yell, "You've never known anything; no one saw anything! No one! No one heard anything! You damned liar!" The accused had apparently answered, trying to defend himself. The voice of the accuser gets even louder, it almost breaks.

It sounds like blows are delivered. "Ow, ow!" I hear a voice crying several times. I become thoroughly frightened.

"Bring in the next one!" someone calls out from the large interrogation room. A GI opens the door. Several officers are sitting at a long table, having a heated discussion. The GI points at me. The presiding officer, presumably Jewish, who barely managed to escape from Germany in time, gives him a sign. Move on. Without exchanging a word, I am led out the other door. Anyway, with what would they have charged me? As an anti-aircraft helper, we thought we were doing our duty by protecting women and children from bombing attacks.

The next day, I am sent home with an American release paper, which was later taken away by the French. Together with others, we run to the train station in Hanau. Piece by piece, I'm getting closer to home, first to Frankfurt and then to Mannheim. I walk over the Rhine Bridge to Ludwigshafen, and again another border checkpoint. We leave the American sector and enter the French sector. We travel to Heuchelheim/Klingen by way of Neustadt, Landau and Rohrbach. I'm getting more excited and more anxious. When I get off the train, I meet Hans Hoffman, a student who had gone to elementary school with me. He's coming back from instruction in Landau. I don't dare ask him whether my mother or my sister is still alive, or if our house is still standing. So, I carry my uncertainties all the way home with me.

I'm, standing in front of the door to my house. It is dark inside. Today is December 23rd, 1945, one day before Christmas. I have been gone for two years now. I left when I was fifteen and a half and return at seventeen and a half. I try to open the front door. It's locked. I cross the street to my grandmother's house. There is still a light on in the kitchen. Quietly, I open the front door and then I open the door to the kitchen. There is my grandmother. As always, she's sitting next to the stove; my cousin Albert is sitting next to her. They must have thought that they had seen a ghost. After some time, they are able to speak. My cousin runs off to call my mother and my sister. They had gone to some neighbors to give each other courage and hope. They can't believe their eyes. They hadn't heard from me for almost a year and didn't know whether I was still alive or not. We were never ones for a big to-do. They asked me what I would like to have. What I want? I want to be able to wash myself with warm water, to finally put on some clean underwear and then go to bed! Do I want something to eat? No, I can't, I'm too excited, too exhausted. They all run to prepare a fresh bed for me, bring me warm water, a clean towel, fresh underwear: one kindness after another! I don't want to relate anything. I can't relate anything. I only want to sleep, sleep and sleep. I fall into bed. My mother tucks me in, and I feel that nothing can happen to me now!

"Tomorrow is Christmas," says my mother as she is leaving. Yes, but there will never be a greater gift than I received today in my entire life.

After Christmas vacation, school started again on January 10th, 1946. With a patched-up bicycle, a balloon tire with patches on the front and a normal wheel with patches on the rear, I ride to school with my friends from Göcklingen. I meet some old classmates again. A few are missing, including Hatzenbühler who shared the school bench with me and was killed during the final months of the war. I've been gone for two years now and missed a lot of schooling, but in its place I received life experience, as well as trust in God. Of course, the price was high!

Finally, let us admit the truth expressed by the old Grandmaster J.W. Goethe. In one of his satirical epigrams, he wrote:

> "To think about and remember sweetly; that is life in its most essential."

Yes, my old friend, you may be right. But until today, I had hardly related anything about my experiences.

By the time Hermann Frech returned home, he found that conditions had markedly changed since his adolescent school days. The Southern Palatinate had been conquered mainly by American forces, and most people there first experienced occupation at the hands of Americans. Where that was the case, circumstances changed very soon. The Palatinate was officially assigned to the French occupation zone by the Berlin Declaration of June 5th, 1945, and confirmed in the Potsdam Agreement of August 2nd 1945.

Already beginning March 30th, American forces began to give up occupation duties to French forces who meant to strengthen their claims to an occupation zone and to reparations from Germany. By the end of April most American forces were gone, and French forces were in full control by the beginning of May.

In Göcklingen, certain houses were requisitioned in order to provide quarters for French soldiers. Orders were issued requiring all households to sweep the streets every morning. All stocks of livestock and foodstuffs were inventoried. Livestock, foodstuffs and clothing were confiscated from a number of families. French and Russian prisoners of war had been quartered in the village; they were now transported away*.

The next few years were hard years. Food and fuel was scarce. Despite the close proximity of the Palatine Forest, French military authorities forbade residents from gathering wood. Foodstuffs and livestock were continuously inventoried, and a proportion were regularly confiscated and sent back to France as part of German war reparations. The winter of 1945-46, when Hermann Frech finally returned home, was especially cold.

Göcklingen, and indeed the entire western part of Germany, remained under Allied military occupation until the founding of the Federal Republic of Germany (West Germany) in 1949. From that point on, Germany resumed full civil administration, and life began to return to normal.

---

*Dr. A. Schirmer, Göcklingen bei Landau/Pfalz. pp. 151, 803-4.

Hermann Frech with the 400 year old church organ in Klingen (near Göcklingen)

Hermann Frech is honored with a certificate for his
50 years membership in the Göcklingen chorus

Epilogue

Hermann Frech

Hermann Frech's life returned somewhat to normal when school opened in Landau on January 10th, 1946. He rode a jury-rigged bicycle about nine kilometers (six miles) to the Otto-Hahn-Gymnasium in order to resume the schooling that the war had interrupted.

After completing school in 1948, he decided to become a teacher and began study at the Pedagogical College. Teachers were in great demand due to the war. In fact, young healthy men had a lot of opportunity due to the high losses the war had inflicted particularly on adult males. There was an accelerated teaching certification program in order to get teachers into the schools, and Hermann needed only four years to complete his training.

On Christmas 1952, Hermann got engaged to Gertraud (Traudl) Eck. She was the daughter of a farmer and vintner in Göcklingen, whose family history there goes back to the year 1350. As an only child, she would inherit her father's estate. After they married in 1953, Hermann began his first teaching assignment in the neighboring village of Klingenmünster. His first child, a daughter Hannelore (today a teacher as well) was born in 1954. A son, Hans (today a psychologist) was born in 1956. Because Traudl's mother was very ill, Hermann was able to transfer to the school in Göcklingen in 1963. In that same year, he began his 45-year-long service as organist in the village's protestant church, and his 40-year service as director of the church choir.

In 1965, Hermann Frech was voted into the local council and served as deputy mayor for 20 years.

The school in Göcklingen was closed in 1969 as eight villages combined to establish a new school – the "Kleines Kalmit" – in nearby Ilbesheim. There he was a part of the school's direction as deputy director. He was served a mentor at the University of Landau for students of History and Evangelical Religion. Beginning in 1985 he took over as deputy director at the "Klingbachschule" in Billigheim-Ingenheim.

In the meantime, his father-in-law had converted his farm entirely into a winery. After his daughter Hannelore married Klaus Hohlreiter, they took over running the winery, which had long evolved into a passion for Hermann. He was actively involved in the winery and to date still plays congenial host to buyers and wine enthusiasts.

Hermann Frech retired in 1991. In that same year he organized the founding of a booster club for the school, and also ended 15 years service as a lay magistrate at the state court in Landau. Upon retirement, he became interested in the history of Göcklingen, including some of its houses and families. He helped organize the design and installation of approximately sixty signs attesting the historicity and significance of buildings and other structures throughout the village. He took an active part in organizing celebrations for Göcklingen's 750 year anniversary in 2004. He was also involved in establishing the concert series "Klingende Kirche" ("musical church") that holds four concerts a year.

In 2004, he was named an "honorary citizen" of the community of Göcklingen, and on December 6, 2011, Kurt Beck, Minister President of German Federal State of Rhineland-Palatinate, awarded him the Medal of Merit.

Politisch und musikalisch aktiv

SÜW/MAINZ: Zwei Südpfälzer mit Landesverdienstmedaille ausgezeichnet

Für ihr herausragendes gesellschaftliches Engagement ehrte Ministerpräsident Kurt Beck am Dienstag Hermann Frech aus Göcklingen und Kurt Gamber aus Böbingen mit der Landesverdienstmedaille in der Mainzer Staatskanzlei.

Kurt Beck ehrte fünf Rheinland-Pfälzer in der Mainzer Staatskanzlei, darunter zwei Südpfälzer: Hermann Frech aus Göcklingen (Dritter von links) und Kurt Gamber aus Böbingen (Zweiter von rechts). FOTO: PRIVAT

Der ehemalige Rektor der Grund- und Hauptschule Ilbesheim, Hermann Frech, engagierte sich über 40 Jahren ehrenamtlich, darunter als Mitglied des Ortsgemeinderats Göcklingen, als Erster Beigeordneter, in der Partnerschaftsarbeit mit der französischen Gemeinde Soucy, als Schöffe am Landgericht Landau, Leiter des evangelischen Kirchenchors und Organist, als Fremdenführer am Bachlehrpfad, Leiter des Arbeitskreises „Ortsjubiläum", beim Aufbau der historischen Schmiede und als Herausgeber der Broschüre „Kleiner Rundgang durch Göcklingen".

Kurt Gamber vertrat von 1974 bis 2005 als Personalratsvorsitzender die Interessen seiner Kollegen am Landgericht Landau. Zudem war er viele Jahre kommunalpolitisch als Mitglied des Verbandsgemeinderats Edenkoben und des Ortsgemeinderats Böbingen engagiert. Mit großer Leidenschaft widmet er sich der Musikpflege beim MGV Hochstadt und MGV Böbingen. Seit 26 Jahren ist er dessen Vorsitzender. Zudem ist er seit 18 Jahren Vorsitzender des Sängerkreises Landau/Sürdliche Weinstraße, zu dem über 100 Chöre gehören. (red)

Hermann Frech (3rd from left) is awarded the Medal of Merit of the German Federal State of Rhineland-Palatinate,December 6, 2011

Die Rheinpfalz, December 7, 2011

www.ingramcontent.com/pod-product-compliance
Ingram Content Group UK Ltd.
Pitfield, Milton Keynes, MK11 3LW, UK
UKHW041921190726
13854UKWH00003B/1368

9 781471 081637